HARBINGER

M. P. Hopkins

H A R B I N G E R

-Memoirs of recovery-

Contents

HARBINGER Copyright 1996 by M. P. Hopkins.
  First printing: October, 1997.
  Second printing: November, 1997.

Permission to use ER document granted by The Hospital of the
University of Pennsylvania Legal Affairs Office, 1997.

Queries regarding *There is a Season*, by Joan Chittister should be
directed to ORBIS BOOKS - P.O. Box 308 - Maryknoll, NY - 10545-
0308. Reprinted by permission of Orbis Books, 1997.

Song written by Stephen Bracciotti from *Cafe des Arts*, copyright
1993. Published by *Tower House Music*; licensed by BMI.
Reprinted by permission of Stephen Bracciotti, 1997.

Lyrics by Natalie Merchant from *Tigerlily*, copyright 1995 Elektra
Entertainment Group, a Division of Warner Communications Inc. for
the United States and WEA International Inc. for the world outside
the United States.

Printed by Odyssey Press Inc., Dover, New Hampshire 1997.
Artwork and Poetry by M. P. Hopkins

ISBN 0-9661525-0-6

To my husband, Christopher,
with love and gratitude.

Acknowledgments

I thank the people who supported me in this effort,
especially Mark and Karen Kotapka in Narberth, Pennsylvania, for
their help and encouragement and concern... and for my life. *What
a long road it has been.*

My family's support has been phenomenal. I thank my
sister-in-law, Stacey Bartling Pydych, and my brother,
Charlie Pydych of Minneapolis/St. Paul, for recognizing the
emergency and for placing the phone call to the ER at HUP and for
their support and encouragement in the years thereafter. I thank
my parents, Charles and Constance Pydych of Valley Forge,
Pennsylvania, for their support, insight and love through a most
difficult and trying time. I thank my brother, Tony Pydych, and his
wife Christine, of Seattle, Washington, for their support and
guidance. Much appreciation to my mother and father-in-law,
Marilyn and Don O'Reilly of Wells, Maine for helping and handling
an unsettling situation with grace. Gratitude to my father-in-law,

John S. Hopkins of Franklin Square, New York, for his promotional efforts, as well as his concern.

I thank those who were, and are on the rehab floor, *Ravdin*, at the Hospital of the University of Pennsylvania, especially Diane Kendall Flores, speech pathology; Christine Motisko, occupational therapy; and Adam DeClerico, physical therapy. Though you've gone to new workplaces and names have changed, there will *always* be a sixth floor in my mind. *Thank you all.* I thank Magee Rehabilitation Services in Philadelphia, Pennsylvania, for their part in this reconstruction... especially Carol, the physical therapist. Thank you to those who are Bayside Rehab in Portland, Maine (...too many to list!) and especially the clients who had a profound effect on me. Thank you to Karen, a physical therapist in the rehab at York Hospital, York Maine.

I thank John N. Cole, author and editor of *Maine Times* in Brunswick, Maine, for all his tremendous support, help and encouragement and the support of the staff of *MAINE IN PRINT* in Brunswick. Thank you all very much. Thanks to Lex Paradis, of Phoenix Publications in Sugar Hill, New Hampshire for editing the first draft of *Harbinger* and for his support, insight and helpfulness. Also, Al Morris, of Phoenix Publications in Kennebunk, Maine, for his knowledge and help.

Thanks to Michael Keating of Ogunquit, Maine for his craft of revision... more than editing, he taught me something about sculpting words. Thank you to Bill Yegge of Wells for his discerning eye, which was helpful in the editing, among other things.

I thank Joann Stover of Jaffrey, New Hampshire for *all* of her incredible support and help. Thank you to Linda and Will Buddenhagen of Ogunquit for their help and support. Thanks to Beverly Bryant of South Paris, Maine for my lessons on self-publishing and Elisabeth C. Pollack also of South Paris, Maine for her help. I thank Suzanne Hobbes of Kennebunkport, Maine for the lessons in writing and life. Thanks to Michael Dion of Wells, Maine for teaching me how to make sense of a computer. I thank Joe Dynan a writer, also of Wells, for his help when I really didn't know where I was heading with all of this. Also, thanks to the staff at Wells Public Library in Wells, Maine, for their help... especially Betsy.

My appreciation to Mary Rich, of Wells, and Vicki Sandini, of Kennebunk, for their support, concern and kindness. Thanks to Jim and Lori Savard of Philadelphia, for their friendship and support. Thank you to Lauren Pollaro and Stephen Bracciotti of York, Maine for their support and friendship.

Special thanks to Daniel P. Finegan ESQ , at the *Law Offices of Obermayer, Rebmann, Maxwell and Hippel* in Philadelphia, for his involvement in this matter and for his concern, kindness and understanding. Also, thanks to Terrence Garmey and Associates at *Smith, Elliot, Smith & Garmey, PA* in Portland, Maine for their involvement and concern.

Much appreciation to Karen McCarthy at Odyssey Press in Dover, New Hampshire for her time and patience.

Finally, I thank Father Paul Coughlin, formerly of Saint Mary's in Wells, Maine... for leading me to the path.

I thank those whose names escape me or perhaps, that I have chosen not to mention. There are volumes in my silence.

HARBINGER

Memoirs of Recovery

I remember once when I was a child, I climbed to the top of the pine tree next to our house to see a birds nest. As I peeked into the nest, the branch I was standing on snapped and I came down about thirty feet. I watched the branches pass as I fell. It was an interesting perspective, falling.

Nothing happened to me. I landed on my back with a thud and I got up, and that was that. I wasn't hurt.

I got up and ran into the house yelling at the top of my lungs, "Dad! I fell from the very top of the pine tree!!!"

"No you didn't," Dad said in a rather unconvinced manner.

"Yes I did!" I retorted.

"No you didn't," Dad repeated, shaking his head from side to side.

"I *did*... I *fell*... from the *very top!*" I said with a little less certainty.

"No you didn't... you didn't fall Maddie."

I guess Dad didn't believe me because I wasn't injured.

I began having dreams I could fly. The dreams seemed so real, just like the fall. I wasn't hurt by the fall so I thought I could fly and I attempted to fly again from the top of the stairs a few weeks later. As it turned out, I couldn't fly. I fell down a full flight of stairs and lost bladder control. But... I *did* fall from the tree.

preface

Last week, my husband and I visited a nursery school which our daughter will attend this September. It's hard to believe she will be starting school. In the visit last week we were invited to witness an entire three hour class. My husband had to leave after an hour as he had appointments at his office, but I was able to stay for the entire session. It was wonderful watching our daughter and all the children interact and learn, remaining silent about my story of birth... and rebirth. I know now because the story is somewhat overwhelming, I have had to keep silent for the implications. The story has to do with my husband, my daughter, myself and our futures and although it may sound mysterious, it is the reality that I have been faced with. This is a story about one life in the vast enormity of time. I communicate this because I have the *ability to do so* and perhaps something good will come from this unveiling.

It all began the moment I was created. It was a mass of tangled blood vessels, a congenital disorder... a birthmark, except it was in my brain. Otherwise known as an *"Arteriovenous Malformation"*. Still, I went through life as an energetic child, then

17

teenager and finally adult. I am not a celebrity, politician, doctor, writer, theologian, minister or scientist. But, I am an artist and designer... and recently I've become a mother. I never wanted the intense struggles of the life that is mine, but now, finally... I see my life as a wonderful gift.

M.P.Hopkins - April 1996

prologue

1992 proved to be the most successful year of my career as a self-supporting architectural designer and painter, although the road leading there was rocky and unclear. The moment I realized I had chosen the wrong major in college *two years* after graduating from Rhode Island School of Design with a major in illustration, I took out another student loan and I went back to school for interior architecture. This time the school was Drexel University in Philadelphia.

I lived in Narberth, a suburb west of the city. At the end of my second semester at Drexel, a friend who worked in corporate design called to let me know a position had opened for an entry level designer at a reputable firm in the city and suggested I give it a try. As I entered the building that day, I knew I was in the right place. The space was open yet, I felt "drawn in" and thoroughly comfortable. I was not qualified for the position academically, so when they turned me down at the end of the interview I told them I would be willing to work with no pay just to get a feel for the environment. Six weeks later, I was on the payroll. There were no tricks involved... I just loved the atmosphere and the challenge.

Born in 1960, I was pretty independent early on in life; I would come up with my own explanations for certain oddities in life. I seemed to need the reasons for *why things are the way they are.* My brother, Charlie dubbed this phenomena *Maddie's theories.* I found it a bit patronizing, or perhaps it was his maniacal laughter. After all, there *is* a reason for almost anything in life.

In December 1987 I moved to northern New England after my husband, Douglas, died in highway collision on the Pennsylvania Turnpike. At the time, I remember someone saying to me, "You will *never* experience this pain again in your life..." It was a consoling thought. My sister, Leslie, and her husband, Kevin, lived in southern Maine and I found a house rental in Eliot, Maine, adjacent to Portsmouth where I worked as a designer in an architectural firm.

Less than a year later, I managed to pull myself up from the devastation of a "corporate-style execution" and was trying to make a new career as a painter on the southern coast of Maine. Losing my career in corporate design simply took the wind out of my sails. What's more, I was let go three days prior to a planned vacation to Europe. To this day, I clearly remember the totally unaffected look in the executioner's eyes as he permanently altered my entire career. The plane and Eurail tickets were non-refundable, so I went. I had nightmares and I cried in my sleep just about every night according to the women in the hostels where I spent the nights during the trip. *Other than that...* the trip was great. When I returned to the states, I worked as a waitress and exhibited my work in several galleries... and I began a relationship with Christopher Hopkins.

Chris was in real estate, a self-made man who knew something about needing independence. He designed his life around his freedom. He was precisely who I wanted in my life. It wasn't just a matter of wanting each other, we needed each other.

In May of 1989, my sister was hospitalized in her sixth month of pregnancy. Her husband told us the doctors diagnosed her condition as a brain disorder known as *arteriovenous malformation*, or A.V.M. Nothing like this had ever happened in our family. My parents, my two brothers and I, as well as the entire family were floored, but I think all of us felt hopeful. I visited my sister in the hospital as much as I possibly could, four or five days a week. Each week, I could see something was different about her, but I wasn't allowed to ask any questions. There was tension in the air. Maybe, that is what happens when two families are forced to share love. Division.

Then, a turn of events. Leslie was rushed down to Massachusetts General Hospital in Boston. I went down too. After a while, three hours to be exact, I realized no one was going to tell me what was happening to my sister, so I went home. It was one of the most bizarre moments in my life. The next day, the baby was

20

born, a cesarean birth. It was a beautiful baby girl.

Also that day, it was revealed Leslie had been misdiagnosed. It was not A.V.M., it was a rare brain cancer, *basal cell melanoma*. Two days later, my sister underwent brain surgery to remove the cancer.

After the operation, Leslie was aware, even through the veil of the drugs. When I looked into her eyes she was right there. I could see she hated what was happening to her. Still, all of my family felt optimistic. Through the entire ordeal, which lasted about six months, I wanted to hold her hand, but I knew she wouldn't want that. I was her little sister, she had always been the strong one.

A few days before she died I was in her hospital room, no one else was there. She was heavily sedated. I put my head gently on Leslie's midsection and I began to cry. I whispered, "It's so unfair... I'm so sorry Leslie...I'm so sorry..."

My sister died on October 5, 1989. It was my birthday.

~ ~ ~ ~ ~ ~

Three months later, my right hand began tingling. I remember thinking how obvious it must be to everyone that this tingling is psychological. I did not want to reveal my medical history because I didn't want to give anyone the impression that it was *all in my head*, but I did. I began working with orthopedic surgeons and therapists and I learned about *over-use syndrome* and *cubital tunnel syndrome*. I was given a wrist brace and was told to limit the use of my right hand.

In January 1990, I was asked to redesign a restaurant in York, Maine. Then, in September that year, I was offered the opportunity to run my own gallery in Ogunquit, Maine, for the summer of 1991.

Chris and I married in September that year and went on our honeymoon after I closed the gallery for the season. We flew down to Siesta Key, Florida (Chris's folks had a house there) where we planned to spend several days at Disney World, a place we hadn't experienced yet. Mid-way through the first day at Disney, my right foot and ankle became completely numb and the entire leg weakened. At the end of the second day the final ride left me light-headed and nauseous. By the time we reached the house, Chris wanted to take me to the hospital but with my recent medical history, I didn't see the point. I felt the doctors would dismiss the problem as psychological again. Everyday of the honeymoon, Chris woke me, I showered and ate, then went back to bed... *to sleep.* I couldn't snap out of it. It was the most unremarkable honeymoon in the history of time. When we got back to Maine, I went to the emergency room and was diagnosed with pneumonia and bronchitis.

~ ~ ~ ~ ~ ~

By January 1992, after seeking the expertise of seven medical professionals in a two year time frame, I asked for a complete physical. After what happened to my sister, I wanted to know what was *wrong* with me. *Something* was wrong. The tingling had traveled from my hand to my shoulder, and to the right side of my back. I also was experiencing tingling in my right foot and ankle, as well as soreness in my left hip, as my entire body was shifting to compensate for the weakness of the right side. My body was twisting before my eyes, my right shoulder was easily an inch higher than the left and my right leg was beginning to *not* want to respond, as if it was exhausted. I laid it all out for the doctor... *What is wrong with me?*

He called me in to go over his findings. He told me could find nothing wrong. He wrote the name of a social worker whom I was to see once a week.

I was commissioned to redesign a four-hundred-thousand dollar home, then another redesign after that. By March I was asked to design an entire building, not a redesign. I completed the design and the construction documents just in time to open my gallery for the second season. I worked on my architectural drawings during slow periods in the gallery.

In August, Chris and I were very happy to learn I was pregnant. At last, I would be a mother! It was a wonderful feeling to know there was a life inside of me, listening to me... not knowing anything about surroundings... or feelings... or people. Simply, not knowing.

I decided to close the gallery at the end of the summer. I

had become friends with the owner of the building so when he asked me to revise the floor plan for the gallery based on his ideas, and a few of mine, I felt a little pang of sadness.   My gallery would become a B&B.

I painted snow scenes on Christmas ornaments which I sold at fairs in November, and redesigned an old supermarket building for a local *Century 21* company.   I was pleased that my pregnancy did not effect my status as a designer.

Chris and I flew down to Siesta Key at the end of the month.   We figured it would be the chance to unwind alone, after all, the baby was due March 15, 1993. I began to feel little flutters in my tummy, then, all-out kicks!

I planned a visit to Philadelphia on Christmas day. My brother, Charlie and his wife Anastasia and their son, Evan would be there from Minneapolis. I wrapped all the presents, a winter hat for Evan, shirts for Charlie and Stacey, a sweater for Dad and I had the perfect gift for my mother. She had a strong belief in fundamental principles of the Far Eastern religions. A weeping Buddha seemed to be the perfect gift for a mother who had lost her first child in 1989 to brain cancer.   Christmas Day, I packed the presents and my things, and Chris drove me down to Logan Airport in Boston. We kissed and hugged, and I boarded the plane.

On December 27, 1992, I woke later than usual after an evening of family reunion. I showered and sat down for breakfast with Charlie, Stacey and Evan.   I heard a key turning in the apartment door and in walked Mom who became a bit miffed at the sight of us eating. We quickly surmised she had planned a meal. In an attempt to rationalize with her I pointed-out the time, and I left the room.

Dad entered the apartment.

A few minutes later, I complained of a headache. Anastasia and I were talking, and I recall speaking strangely.

~ ~ ~ ~ ~ ~

23

HOSPITAL OF THE UNIVERSITY OF PENNSYLVANIA
OPERATIVE REPORT

PATIENT'S NAME: **HOPKINS, Madeleine**
CHART NUMBER: 1033360-7
DATE OF OPERATION: **12/27/92**
PREOPERATIVE DIAGNOSIS: **Spontaneous intracerebral hemorrhage**
POSTOPERATIVE DIAGNOSIS: **Same (possible arteriovenous malformation)**
OPERATION: Craniotomy for ICH
SURGEON: **Kotapka**   ASSISTANT: **Lasner**
ANESTHESIA: General endotracheal
ESTIMATED BLOOD LOSS: 700 cc   REPLACED: None

INDICATIONS: The patient is a 32-year-old female near the end of her second trimester of pregnancy who was brought to the emergency room of the Hospital of University of Pennsylvania comatose. Emergency CT scan demonstrated a large left parietal intracerebral hemorrhage extending to the ventricular system, which was filled with blood. There was also acute hydrocephalus. From the CT scanner she was taken emergently to the operating room without delay.

PROCEDURE: After positioning her supine on the operating table with head turned toward the right, a curvilinear scalp incision was made extending from the zygoma superiorly and curving anteriorly to end behind the frontalmost

---

portion of this incision, a single hole was placed with the twist drill and an emergent ventriculostomy was placed into the frontal horn with egress of spinal fluid under markedly elevated pressure. This was drained to less that 10 cm of water, following which attention was turned to the remaining portion of the craniotomy. A scalp flap was reflected. Raney clips were applied to the edges. The temperalis muscle was incised with the bovie and also reflected. A single burr hole was placed at the superior posterior aspect of the exposure and the a circular bone flap approximate 7 cm in diameter was turned and elevated. The dura was then opened at its superior- and posteriormost portion. Brain under severely high pressure was encountered. A corticectomy was made in this location at a point at which the brain was obviously blue and discolored from the underlying hematoma. The hematoma cavity was encountered and a huge hematoma was aspirated with suction and aid of irrigation. At the depths of the hematoma cavity there was encountered some reddish-tannish, very friable and vascular tissue which had the appearance of an arteriovenous malformation.....

Mark J. Kotapka, M.D.

MJK/jjb

Beginning Again

The following chapter represents entries of a journal
kept by
Christopher M. Hopkins

1

Pulling the Clip

Tues. 29th Dec. 1992
Nurse: Sarah

    Madeleine slept fairly well during the night. High stimulation once or twice, was given morphine to calm her down.
    CT scan midmorning, again morphine. Dr. Kotapka saw her & reported to me and family Madeleine showed a little improvement which was "optimistic." More eye opening & improved response to pain & stimulus.
    Physical therapist arrived & O.T. soon to be arriving. Showed me how to stretch her Achilles tendon to reduce overtoneness. To be done 3xdaily.
    Madeleine is well sedated so that may add to her not coming around just yet. When she does come around sedation may cause her to speak irrationally & possibly hallucinate.

Late afternoon Madeleine is resting. O.T. was in to do a few tests. Madeleine was stiffer this morning. She opened her eyes for quite a few seconds, perhaps 10 - 15 seconds.

Rest well honey, see you later.

Tues. night
Nurse: Becky

You seem to be more rambunctious tonight, perhaps a bit more than is good for you. Blood pressure goes up which brings on the morphine. 2mlg 1st - 5 mins. later 2 more and after about 12 mins. total, it kicked in, and you settled down.

They need to keep you calm while you heal. Heal baby, heal. Just don't be frightened honey, we're going to get through this just fine. Time is on our side.

Good night. I love you.

Dec. 30, 1992
Wed. 4 - 5 AM

Cat scan & baby check ok. Having difficulty breathing. Taking Madeleine for check for possible blood clot in lung, then perhaps excessive fluid. She has been given a diuretic to perhaps alleviate that.

Note: unit bag of hemoglobin given to Madeleine Tues. night.

Wed. 6AM.

Pulmonary embolism check is low probability. Extra body fluid could be due to transfusion. After diuretic & release of greater volume of urine & release of fluids in lung cavities Madeleine's blood pressure dropped. Her oxygen level is better but she is being given dopamine to increase her blood pressure. She needs to stabilize.

Note: theoretic possible heart problem but at this time no evidence of that.

Hang in there Madeleine, be strong.

7:30 AM
     Madeleine appears to be stabilizing. Thank you, Lord.
Her oxygen level is good & blood pressure getting stronger.
As it increases, she will be weaned of the dopamine. No
signs of heart trouble and OB says baby is still doing fine.
Cause of labored breathing and resulting fluid overload
unknown. Possibility: clogged tube.
     Dear God, stay with her.

Later...
     Visits short & quiet, family members only.
Madeleine doing better. Vital signs look good. Last night
troubles seem to be blocked tube after all. (Blockage in
breathing airway.)
     Charlie, Connie and Tony visited before and after lunch
@ museum.
     Madeleine doing well right through evening into the night.
4 occasions of sedation. Breathing set at 50% assisted 50%
Madeleine.
        Goodnight my love   xoxoxoxo

Thurs. Dec. 31, 1992
     Happy New Year! I've declared this year, 1993, to be the
"year of our baby, the three of us, our family." You've had a
pretty good night so far, resting well. When I came in to say
my goodnight you opened your eyes right away even though
you were so relaxed. Your recognizing made me so happy...

Fri. Jan. 1, 1993
     ...you've got a small infection it seems from the ventilator.
Temp.is up and also the baby's heartbeat. After culture
result is back then probably an antibiotic. I'll keep an eye on
this for you.
     Good job pulling the clip off your finger [blood pressure].
You knew exactly how to do it.

33

Fri. night
    Becky is with you tonight & she's taking good care of you. You seem to be lighter & more determined to pull out plugs, wires, etc... a good sign but just take it easy until Monday. Just two more days. Then hopefully no ventilator. You should be getting antibiotic in AM after OB/Gyn visit & we'll nip that bug in the nose. Rest peacefully & have patience.
                      I love you, Goodnight

    P.S. Lauren says "hi".

Sat. Jan. 2, 1993
    ...everyday is a busy day for you. Off you went on another field trip this morning. Routine Cat scan & x-ray which says you're still doing fine... Possible indication that maybe this second drainage valve going in on Monday could be the last. Hopefully no shunt...

Sat. eve.
    I'm not sure but it seems like you just followed a couple commands & your eyes seemed to follow my voice. A real good feeling...

Sat. night late -
    ...open eyes alot now. That's good. I just hope you can get good night's rest with your fever. Your temp. is up but Dr.Lasner just saw you & he is more concerned with your oxygen level. It seems better now. Blood sugar is a little off so, you got a dab of insulin. Baby's heart rate is good considering the fever. 148 BPM. Your nurse, Diane, is giving you a "cool comfort" and that, along with some Tylenol should help bring your temp. back down a little. I think the heat is keeping you restless. Just hang tight honey. Let's be patient & strong & we'll get you though this. Thank you Lord for all you've done.
    I love you Madeleine!
                  Good night...

Sunday January 3, 1993
> *They're switching you to phenobarbital... Lori & Jim & Aunt Nancy were by to say hello. Lori drove my car down from Maine. I hate to leave but our lives back home are kind of up in the air... rest for now and get that temperature down.*

Sun. night
> *I just said goodnight and I know you heard me. Please have patience for this most difficult journey. It worries me to see you frightened... but I must say, you are doing much better. Your eyes are following more, you are using that right arm more often and you seem to be closer to this world's awareness. I wish I could know what's going on inside your mind. Maybe then I could help more to alleviate your fears and frustrations. I'm going to just go by my intuitive feelings and do everything I can to make this burden on you lighter in every way. With my trust in God, the doctors and you, I know you will soon heal and we will walk from these halls together.*
> *God bless you honey and rest well.*

> > > *I love you   xoxo*

Monday January 4, 1993
> *Temperature is high, 105 and therefore, agitation and blood pressure changes. Rapid swings from high to low agitation's.*

12:30 - 1:00 - Temp. is down to 102. Agitation less severe. It must be exhausting for you. Hopefully, you will rest and settle down.

5:00 PM - Your temp. is settling, it seems... and you are resting easier. If you have a good night I will be heading to Maine to take care of things onTues. A.M., and will be back as soon as I can. Probably Thurs.
> *I played Van the Man for you, hope you enjoyed it...*

Thurs. 1/7/93

> *Back to Philly. Madeleine alert again, or at least opening eyes more. They also seem clearer. Busy day lined up for Fri. You've got your casts and splint on. The casts are intended to keep your ankle tendons flexible.*

> *I think we're both tired so goodnight honey and I'll see you in the morning.*

Fri. Jan. 8, 1993

> *You've been sitting up in a chair this morning for close to four hours... you even got to bend your knees. That must have felt good. This afternoon you're going on a field trip. It's trachiostomy time. I know it doesn't sound like much fun but I think you'll be a lot more comfortable... It's time to start waking up more. I had a dream last night that you had started talking when people were "yapping" around your bed. I had to get them to pipe down because you had something to say but they were too busy talking and you couldn't get a word in edgewise. It was kind of funny, but I was so excited that you were talking...*

Fri. night-

> *It's so nice to see your face again. [It had been contorted due to the tubes protruding out of the mouth and down the throat.] Tracheostomy went well & your mouth is free of all intrusions. It looks much more comfortable.*
> *Tonight has been fairly quiet although you did reach up and grab a pad & hose. Good sign.*

Midnight - Your drain has been changed. At 6AM you've got another field trip, CAT scan. If all goes well & you are draining on your own accord then celebrate, no shunt. That's where my prayers are going tonight. Now, I've got to sleep, I'm pretty tired. I'll see you in the morning. Good night, Honey.

> > > *I love you   xoxo*

Sat. Jan 9, 1993

Good morning, Madeleine. So far, so good. Your exam supports keeping the ventriquolostomy clamped. This is good. You also seemed much brighter. I've even seen you yawn for the first time. Now we need to get you cooled down a bit. You're still at 102. Doesn't look to me that there is much to watch. Oh well.

Dr. Langer thought you might have mouthed something in response to a question. I hope he's right. It'll be great to hear your voice again.

Late night- You've just closed your eyes to sleep, but they were wide open for a long duration. I must say, you did not look very pleased about where you are, but I'm not sure if that is what you were thinking.

Good night honey...

Sun. Jan 10, 1993
Afternoon.

Everyday is a busy day. Doctors' switched your I.V. lines from the right side of your chest to the left side. Right side was getting irritated. Then, you were up, out of bed between 1:30 & 3:00. I'm not sure you like it but it is good for your circulation. You've been restless and/or awake for most of the day. I try my best to comfort you.

It seems you have a case of bronchitis, most probably from the tube being in your throat. It may be the cause of your temperature spiking. They'll be giving you an antibiotic (okay for the baby) which should clear that up for you.

Honey, you mouthed some words today & I think you said "I love you." It seemed you repeated it after I said it to you. Please have patience and so will I.

Monday, Jan. 11, 1993

It's moving day! You're going to the 9th floor. Neuro recovery floor. I'm off to unemployment today.

*4:00 P.M. - Here we are in room 914. I need to go bring my
things up here since we're now off the 5th floor. We'll
have to say good bye to Sara.*

*Here on the 9th floor, tonight Jim will be taking care of
you & then switch again at midnight. It seems there will be
three 8 hour shifts a day. Your temperature has gone up
again today & there seems to be another infection showing
up in your urine. We'll find out tomorrow. Jim just brought
in a cot for me...*

Good night my love xoxo

Tues. Jan. 12, 1993 AM

*Boy, tough sleeping around here. I'll just have to
adjust. With this cot I'm sleeping on, we'll both need rehab
to walk again...*

*Infection located & antibiotic to start for urinary tract
infection. Temp. still between 101 - 102. Can't figure it out
exactly. With communication between Dr. Kotapka,
nutrition team & OB/Gyn decision made to insert the
feeding tube through nose into stomach. I was told it would
be minimum risk to baby. X-ray needed to feed tube &
make sure it goes in correctly.*

Wed. Jan. 13, 1993

*Well your temp. came down during the night.
Hopefully, it will stay there.*

*Field trip # who knows! They want to make sure your
feeding tube was in correctly. You were sleeping at !:30
but when I got back at 3:00 you were wide awake. The
most responsive I have seen you yet. I feel much better
after seeing you smile. Thank you Lord, and all who have
prayed.*

Sat. Jan. 16, 1993

*I'm starting to communicate with you through eye
contact and some mouthing of words, although I must
admit I'm not very good at reading lips. Also, there's a
good chance that what you're saying may not make*

sense...

So much is happening, it's always busy.
-PT & OT were here Thurs. & Fri...
-Thurs. new casts...
-Fri. sitting up...
-They'll be back on Mon.
-Sat. Kelly, a different PT got you to sit up in a chair,
which was great, except she left, and after about an hour, I
was finished. It was difficult keeping you sitting upright.
You kept sliding off the chair.

Sun. Jan. 17, 1993

It's now 3 weeks. Jim & Lori came today. It's been one
week since they've seen you, and they say you look so
much better. Good to hear. It's tougher when you're here
everyday, through all the ups and downs.

You've got this terrible bed rash honey & I've been
trying all day to get it addressed. Now that you have
sterile sheets   & cortisone ointment, hopefully, that will
do the trick...

Feb. 6, 1993

It feels odd writing again, almost like living in the past...
and this recent past I don't want to relive. The last 2 1/2
weeks have been hectic. The battle continued against
your   rash, fever, etc... and all the ups and downs of the
hospital world. Even with the best doctors', I can't
imagine anyone going through this without 24 hour
watch. So, that is what we've been busy doing. "We"
being your Mom, Dad & myself.

I went back to Maine at the end of Jan. for a few days.
On Sunday night January 31, 1993, I called the Hospital &
your Mom said there was someone who wanted to say
"hello" to me. Your voice was like music to my ears. I'll
never forget that moment.

Needless to say, I left in a snowstorm first thing in the

39

morning, which has led to this past week. So much improvement. You had labor pains, but your fever finally broke. Hallelujah!

The first week of Feb. brought the commencement of real food, the termination of I.V.'s & the capping of your trach to help you talk... and talking, we have been. Talking, laughing & crying...

Stuck Inside

I'm in here.
Doesn't seem like it,
          but, I'm in here.

Won't you help me out?
Won't you help me find
          myself again?

I think I came from
          over there...
Or, maybe it was over there,
          or,
or,

                    or...

Guide me back.
I got lost...
          and
I can't find my way back.

I am in here!

I am.

2

A Different Perspective

I found myself in a room with full-height windows overlooking a field of snow, but I didn't know where I was. Chris was wheeling a cart into the room. In the cart were clothes and I recognized many articles of clothing, as mine. I was trying desperately to get my bearings. There were also things foreign to me, such as a box of surgical gloves. I asked Chris why they were there; he told me they were for "cleaning-up."

"................*Me?*" I asked.

"Yes," he said without hesitation.

"I'm.............. sorry."

I was shocked and stupefied and I didn't understand what was happening with every moment that passed. There was no fluidity in my speech... or my thoughts. I simply could not get my words out, as if they were blocked by my own mouth.

"Don't apologize... it's okay," he said.

Quite suddenly, I realized that I had just come out of a state of being unaware. I wondered how long I had been like that? A few days perhaps?

Chris said something about meeting my *speech therapist* and suddenly, we were on our way. I was in a wheelchair and I knew how to use it. In other words, I had been here... where-ever "here" was, for a while, maybe a week? I didn't know.

Suddenly, a thought came *into my mind from nowhere. A memory of someone showing me how to use a wheelchair. I had no idea who the person was... or when it was... or where it was... but I knew it had happened.*

I realized, *every second* that something was terribly wrong, but I didn't seem to know what it was that was so terribly wrong. It seemed that every five seconds, I would grasp something about the change that had happened but I couldn't hold the thought for more than five seconds. Every minute, I kept trying to get a handle on this *altered state*. There were no thoughts other than that. There were no concepts of anything on a large scale; it was total introspection.

I was introduced to a woman named Diane Kendall. Immediately, I thought about Janet Kendall, my childhood friend and next-door neighbor. Diane gave me a red notebook and I thanked her. On the cover of the notebook, she taped a schedule, but it was not obvious to me why she put it there. I saw numbers indicating times of day but it still wasn't clear to me what she was doing. Nothing was relevant in my mind. Next to the schedule, was a note that read:

> PT: Adam
> OT: Chris
> Speech: Diane
> Recreational: Tracey
>   Jeannie
> Social Work: Lisa

I was confused about what it all meant. What did "PT" or "OT" mean? What was Chris's name there for? There was little comprehension and I knew that. Every minute, the revelation that I had lost my mind became excruciatingly apparent. I thought I had a mental breakdown, but no one had told me. My *intelligence* was different, but I couldn't remember *how* it was different. I couldn't remember anything about who I had been. Additionally, I couldn't recall my age.

The first page of the notebook was a calendar, specifically, the month February 1993. *February?* Then, I looked at the numbers *1993*. *How could it be 1993?* I realized I could not place myself in time. *What a strange feeling*, I thought.

On the eighth day of the month, the word "REHAB" was written. Diane explained to me that day, was today. I was tremendously confused. It seemed I had no concept of time. It seemed I had lost twenty years of my existence. I simply could not remember anything about my life, in any kind of order.

The second page of the notebook was also the second section, titled "ORIENTATION." On this page, Diane wrote:

HOSPITAL OF THE

UNIVERSITY OF

PENNSYLVANIA

FEBRUARY

1993

This is where I was born... Hospital of the University of Pennsylvania... What am I doing here? How did I get here? What happened to me? Diane went on to write:

CAME TO HOSPITAL
DECEMBER 27, 1992

SURGERY ON HEAD
DECEMBER 27

REHAB FEB 8

Silently, I scanned what she had written. There was no memory of anything.

*Surgery on head? What does **that** mean?* I thought. *Uh-oh... Uh-oh... What has happened? What has happened to me?*

My first inclination was to touch my head, but I didn't for fear of what I might find. The one thing I was able to keep in mind was total disbelief that this was actually occurring. It was so bizarre, it was beyond my comprehension. I thought it would be best to just listen to what she had to say. She continued writing, and I knew that I was supposed to put it all together, yet everything she was writing was unfamiliar to me. Over and over, I tried remembering the day but there was no recollection of the day or even the knowledge that I had planned any trip. On the fourth page, Diane wrote:

```
December 27, 1992 - Surgery
            to
January 1993 - Asleep
            to
January 8 - Trach in Neck
            to
Jan 13-not talking-no eye contact
            to
February 1 - Up in chair
            to
February 9 - To Rehab
```

*What **is** this?* I thought.

Although, the clarity of what she had written seemed clear to her, to me it wasn't. I knew she treated me "differently," like something was not right. As a matter of fact, I seemed to know that something had happened to me, simply by the way she talked to me, related to me and responded to me. The thing was, I was not able to remember anything about who I had been. I didn't recall yesterday or last week. I couldn't recollect anything about who I was or where I came from, or just about anything in my life. I was unable to re-member my age, either.

Suddenly, out of nowhere I remembered waking from a nap and feeling very rested... incredibly untroubled. It was some kind of flashback. In that instant, my mind and body felt so sheltered, and I wondered why? It was odd. It was addictive: I did not want it to end. It seemed, that I had been gently laid there, as if I had fallen from a cloud. There were

47

no disturbances, all was calm. It was very nice. There was
something there... with me, too... but I couldn't fathom what
it was. It wasn't a person, but it kept me... calm.

I was looking for some sign that would place me in time. Then, I forgot what I had just been thinking. I noticed immediately, that I was unable to control my thoughts. I tried to rationalize, then I would forget what I had been trying to reason. I noticed that I could not stop trying to be objective, even though I was unable to recall what I had just been pondering. When I tried to remember what I was just contemplating, I was unable to retrieve the concept. In my mind, there was no reverse, only forward.

The minute I thought about it, the horror of what Diane had just revealed to me, was gone. The next moment, I sat there with a tear stained face trying to recollect why I had cried. There was no memory. If not for the notebook, I would forget anything... *anyone* had said. I had false confidence which I carried with me at all times.

The meeting with Diane that day, marked the beginning of my new life. Later that afternoon, in my room, Chris and I talked about how I got to Philadelphia, and what had happened prior to February 8, 1993.

"How.............. did.......... I.................... get... .... here?"

"Christmas day, I drove you to Logan", he said. I didn't know it was Christmastime or what *"logan"* was. After a pause, I asked.

"................logan?"

"Logan airport, in Boston. Do you remember?"

"................No," I replied, shaking my head. I was puzzled at my inability to recall this.

Chris nodded. There was no memory of a flight... or a drive to Boston. *Why would I drive to Boston?*, I asked myself. I live.......... That moment, I couldn't remember where I lived.

Chris told me I was staying at my parents' apartment when "it happened". I searched my memory for something... *anything*, to jog my recollection, but there was nothing.

After a pause, he continued saying Charlie, Stacey and

Evan were also visiting.

I was trying to remember who these people were.

Charlie is my brother...

.......and Stacey is his wife... but, Evan?

.......Evan? Oh, Evan is their **son**........ *That's odd, I forgot about Evan.*

__Immediately, I was__ placed in the scene, but it seemed to be unfamiliar. I didn't recognize the place but then, in the blink of an eye, it became clear the setting was my parents apartment in Philadelphia. My brother, Charlie had made breakfast for Stacey and I, when the sound of keys jingling... very clearly, at the apartment door were heard. My mother entered the room and became quite irate at the scene. Unbeknownst to us, she had intended to make breakfast.

"Mom........... was........... angry," I said.

"Why was she angry?" Chris inquired.

I knew the answer to Chris's question, but I couldn't formulate the words to answer his question. I knew it was because she had just come from the store with the intention of preparing breakfast for us but I couldn't effectively communicate this. The problem with not finishing a statement, is in the conjecture issue. I had to try to make it clear that no one was to blame for my condition. Communicating that, in itself was quite an undertaking because I *couldn't*. As much as I tried the words simply would not come out. All I could say was *"No,"* while shaking my head from side to side.

"You know that you're pregnant, right?" Chris asked.

__Abruptly, I was__ thrust into a memory. I only focused on what was directly before me, the details of the scene were not relevant. There was no sense of place or time: I was floating in space. In this memory, I was drifting with no destination. A man came to see me... a nice man. He stayed with me.. a lot, and I began to have feelings for him. I thought he worked wherever it was that I was. After a while, perhaps a week, the man asked me if I knew who he was.

"No", I said shaking my head.

"I am Chris, I'm your husband."

My husband? I don't know this man! He told me I was in the seventh month of pregnancy. I was confused and embarrassed. I did not remember anything about this man, or my pregnancy. I looked down at my belly which was quite large. I was frightened. I thought I was a child, perhaps eight years old. I had no memory of this man but somehow, unlike other men, was not scared by his presence. As a matter of fact, I had wonderful feelings whenever I saw him. I thought I had a crush on him. Still, I was bewildered at this information.

"Madeleine, do you remember where we met?"

I couldn't recall anything about him, or a life with him. Just an incredible blank.

"Do you remember Piper's?" he asked.

Suddenly, visions of different faces from out of my memory... and at first I didn't know where I was. Not an old movie, not a re-run. It was like watching a movie for the first time, I didn't know what to expect. But then, I began to recognize this place, and there in my memory... was Chris. I looked at Chris in astonishment, and he, at me.

"Yes................ I..................... remember," I nodded taking in the new found memory like a treasure from the deepest part of my mind.

"Do you remember the Bethel Inn?"

I didn't know what he was talking about, but I knew he was trying to make a connection.

"Do you remember the pool at the Bethel Inn? We were swimming in the dark with the steam from the warm water all around? I carried you through the water... Do you remember?"

*I closed my eyes, listening to Chris's words, and just like turning on a light, suddenly, the memory was there. It seemed it had been lost for a very long time, because it was unclear, and foreign. But, there was Chris, in my flashback... and I **knew** him. Suddenly, I knew all about him. His laughter... his kindness... his love.*

I looked up at him. My eyes filled with tears. It was unbelievable. What's happened to me? How could I have forgotten this? But I didn't forget. It was there, in the caverns of my mind.

"Do you remember Leslie?"

I nodded immediately. My sister.

"Do you remember Leslie died?"

A cloud of confusion hung low before me. Hospital rooms... and angry faces... and Leslie laying in the bed... and angry faces... and waiting ... and angry faces... I nodded.

"Madeleine, do you remember Doug?"

There was a pause, and I looked down. I nodded.

Douglas was my husband. Doug died in a highway accident on the Pennsylvania Turnpike in 1986. I felt the black curtain descending on me.

My mind was altered, and I felt as if I couldn't deal with the new one. I didn't know this new one, it was alien. I couldn't recall how my mind worked from one minute to the next. I only hoped that I had been an honest person because I was unable to remember anything about the person who's body I was in.

What has happened to me? Please tell me!

"On Christmas day, you flew down to see your parents and brother. You went into a coma at about 2:00 PM on the 27th, 1992. You came out of the coma on January 31, 1993."

"Yes........... I........... know." Everything he said, I knew... but how could I have known? There was no recollection of a specific moment when this was revealed to me, but somehow I *just knew*. Within seconds, the memory and the content of the discussion was gone.

At any time, whether I willed it or not, memories of faces and conversations came to mind, then vanished. But it wasn't every once in a while, *it was every five seconds*. I was filled with an over-whelming pain of the loss of my mind and an equally devastating fear of what lay ahead.

Suddenly, I noticed my right arm had *no feeling*. My fingers were grossly swollen and lifeless. My whole right side was unmanageable and more than weak... it was *powerless*. Again, out of nowhere I remembered a moment of indescribable confusion and utter desperation. Somehow, I knew it was the moment I had woken

51

from the coma. But then, the reality of waking changed from something pleasant *(... gently fallen from a cloud...),* to a horrific *surreality.*

> *What has happened to me? It's my right hand! Oh! Not my right hand! Not my right arm! What has happened??? There was a voice inside my mind that always answered, "Hold on... Hold on... Hold on..." I cried for the loss; it was so much. I knew I had lost myself. It was the death of the person I had been.*

Chris could see I was exhausted, yet it was so early in the day. Even my ability to stay awake was gone. He raised the safety bars around my bed. I objected, then realized it was necessary; it was only my pride that was caged.

~ ~ ~ ~ ~ ~

Chris woke me and helped me to freshen-up. I wondered what day it was, and why I was here. I wondered what time it was, I looked out the window, *It's daylight.*

A woman was in the room, too. The woman helped me with my shoes. I didn't recognize the shoes, yet they were mine. White high-top sneakers. *Where did they come from,* I thought. The woman laced one shoe, then the other. She reached into the sneaker and pulled out a wad of tissue and began laughing loudly. There was something familiar about her laugh. Chris and I laughed too. I wanted to know how long I had been walking around with a wad of tissue in this shoe. Suddenly, it wasn't funny to me anymore. I couldn't feel my foot. My right foot.

"Connie, I'll be back in a minute," Chris said.

Connie!? The woman was my *mother! This happened before*, I thought. *Why can't I remember my mother?*

Chris placed several framed photos on the window ledge in addition to "get-well" cards and flowers. One of the photos was Chris and I... on our wedding day, seemingly insignificant... but not. I remembered at some point in time, I was shown the photo but didn't recognize the scene, or Chris. As matter of fact, if it were not

for this photograph, I would not have known anything about my life with Chris. There were two other people in the image but I didn't know who they were either. Yet, this had been my wedding day. I didn't know when it was or where it was. This was the evidence. I had a life.

Chris wheeled me down the hall to a dining area. There were fifteen or twenty people in the room wearing robes.

They all have the same problem as me... I thought

Chris placed a plate in front of me, and began cutting the food into small pieces. I realized I was unable to use the utensils with both hands. My right hand had no strength... and nothing was logical. Chris said he would be back momentarily, I nodded.

Suddenly, a woman who I knew came in the dining hall. I was trying to place her...

She and I worked in a frame shop in Narberth, Pennsylvania a long time ago... I couldn't place the time, maybe twenty years? Or maybe...

I wondered how she knew I was here. I felt self-conscious. I didn't know where I was, but *she* knew I was here. She mentioned something about an appointment with her O.B., and that she thought it would be nice to say "hello". Then, just like the wind, she was gone.

Something really horrible had happened. I couldn't get a grip on reality. What's more, I couldn't *remember* that I couldn't get a grip on reality. From one minute to the next, I could not recall *anything* I had just been thinking. Yet, memories of traumas I had faced flashed before my eyes in an unprovoked manner, and it was non-stop and overwhelming. It was like being put in a room with images of my life before me, mostly the *fearful moments*. The retractions were fresh, as if I had recently experienced them. At the same time, I was not able to retain anything I had just said or what was said to me, with the exception of a handful of moments in time. When my mind was able to hold information, I became briefly aware, then I would "go into the cave" again. The impact of my fragility was *staggering*. Sounds, voices and noises were too intense. My mind was different, immature, unaware... like a scared child... but it was *me*.

54

After dinner that night, Chris wheeled me back to my room and helped me get ready for bed. I was unable to undress myself, and suddenly I realized how ridiculous I felt.

"I'll......... do........... it."

My body was stiff and unyielding and I was trying to remember how to get my clothes off.

Chris helped me with the toothpaste.

I wondered who had taken care of my teeth.

"Who............ brushed.............. my........................ teeth?"

"No one."

I was appalled at the thought of not brushing my teeth for such a lengthy period of time. Suddenly, I had another memory.

> *"Put this in your mouth, it will cleanse your teeth."*
> *"Mmmmmmm................" I said.*
> *"You like that! Must taste nice!" Chris said.*
> *I nodded and smiled.*

I didn't know why I was there, and I didn't know from where I came . There was very little awareness, although I needed to know what happened to me. All those with whom I had contact were unable to explain my condition. I wasn't able to tell anyone... *even Chris*, that I was not able to comprehend what had happened. I was in a state of cerebral elevation and the terror at the inability to reason or understand what had happened was totally over-whelming. I couldn't stop it. I was falling, with no end in sight. The abyss...

Chris wheeled me down the hall to the office of the woman I had seen a few days ago. She used my name each time she spoke but I could not remember hers. She asked me to count, which seemed so simple but I couldn't. She asked me to recite the alphabet, but I couldn't. *Why can't I do this?* Suddenly, I realized she was wearing a name tag. *Diane Kendall. Why didn't I notice her name tag? It was right there!* Diane asked me to write my name, and handed me a pen, but I couldn't remember what the letters were... or how to make them. *This is not good. What's happened? She'll tell me... I'll just wait.*

At the end of the session, Diane wrote in my notebook. It

bothered me that she was writing for me. I looked at what was written in the last session and I realized it hadn't been a few *days* since I last saw Diane. It had been just a few *hours*.

There were moments when I thought I was eight... within a moment, I would think I was twenty-five. Due to the memory impairment I was unaware of the extent of the damage, as I would forget everything within seconds. There was no control of the direction my mind would take. It was on fast forward, then rewind, then fast forward again. I couldn't make it stop or at least pause for a spell. It was relentless and exhausting. Over and over, I seemed to know that I had lost myself. It was totally overwhelming. People would ask me, "Why are you crying?" I had died. That was why... *and I knew that.*

I kept contemplating, *What happened to me?* But I couldn't formulate the words to ask the question. I thought someone would tell me soon... so, I just waited. What's more, I didn't know where I was or the fact that I was even in a *hospital.* I kept having flashbacks of people whom *I didn't know.* It would happen as Chris was talking to me, or other people, when he would *refer* to someone. Specific names, such as *Melissa, Dan, Dr. Kotapka, Dr. Lasner, Sarah, Dr. Langer* and others... I realized these were the people who had been helping me, wherever I was.

I recognized I was completely at the mercy of the people around me, and I was alarmed at my vulnerability. The fact that I was not able to "get-away" from danger... from situations... from *people*... was extremely troubling. I knew that I had to "lay-low" and I realized this feeling was not a paranoia, but somehow based on my own experiences in life... and in the hospital.

I knew hazardous situations immediately. I was in the care of people who knew nothing about my life, about my past... and I began to remember how I had fought for my dignity so many times in life. But, now I couldn't talk... or run... but maybe I could still scream. Then, I realized that wouldn't work either. I had better just lay-low.

Chris was able to read my eyes and expressions. Like the game of charades, we communicated but there was no *verbal* communication. Unfolding this new side of each of us was like an adventure, and at times intriguing. Chris was so patient with me... and kind. My frustrations were limitless, yet he remained steady and optimistic. I had surges of memory constantly, and he worked with me to let the pieces fall into place... just like a jig-saw puzzle. Chris would try to complete the images. Most of the time, the recollections were reflective of human kindness... but not always.

Anger

*You do **not** realize that...*
*I **am** important!*
*I **was** important!*
*I **had** a life!*

    *a **life**...*

*You wonder **why I cry?***
*Well, as soon as I can **talk**,*

You
  will
    be
      the
        first
          to
            know
              why I cry!

Then, you will know.
*And I will **say** to you...*
    ***I'll** say...*
    ***How** could you...*
    ***What** gives you the...*

        ...good-bye

I began having flashbacks of a man who had come to see me, but there was nothing to gauge where or when I had seen him. Not only did I wonder who *he* was, I wondered who *I* was. I knew I had seen him before I had come down to Earth on February 8... and I remembered there was something he had said to me about why I was there, wherever I was. Something that he said told me, *This man is important, he knows something about what happened to me. Perhaps, I will get information from him.* The problem was, I couldn't get hold of anything that he had said. I *understood*, but as soon as he finished speaking, I completely forgot what he had said. I couldn't even remember his name once he finished talking, but I got the *essence* and in my mind, there was a bond with him. I felt that I knew him, although I had never seen him before.

I was unable to communicate and I didn't know why. It was endlessly frustrating. I had so many questions, but I couldn't formulate the words to ask. *I couldn't make words.* Those around me kept silent about what had happened; my condition was a mystery to me.

The rehab floor was known as "Ravdin." One of the first things I realized was that I was wearing a protective undergarment, which is always somewhat disconcerting. I was embarrassed and humiliated but left with a clear realization. I thought about the chimps on "National Geographic Specials" on PBS, wearing their little diapers. As distressing as it was, there must not have been a choice. Until Ravdin, I had basically no memory with the exception of a few moments in time. I knew this meant I must not have been aware up to that point. In my mind, I questioned who had been taking care of things like that. It was Chris.

Everyday was structured to the hour. I would spend an hour in the A.M. and an hour in the P.M. with Diane everyday. The only thing was, I was unaware of the fact that I was spending two hours a day with her. Every time I saw her it felt like I hadn't seen her for a few days. There was also physical and occupational therapy, but the therapy with the most impact for me, was speech. Speech therapy involved all of the cognitive deficits, and although I couldn't figure out Diane's position, I knew whatever it was that she did, was helping me in a big way.

My sense of time was completely distorted. I couldn't remember a schedule for the life of me. Chris would wheel me down to Diane's office at the appropriate time, then return, accordingly. It didn't matter what method was presented to me, I would still forget, or maybe it was constantly losing sight of the *big picture*. Diane and Chris called my condition *"a bleed,"* but I had no idea what that meant. I remember speech therapy, and it was often times extremely upsetting because everything I did reflected the outcome of the bleed. Everyday was another rude awakening. Of course, the therapists' have seen it all, and I would get a great deal of encouragement from their lack of concern; I was no different than any other patient. It left me feeling that everything was okay.

Everyday, Diane mentioned "the baby" and every time, my stomach filled with butterflies and my mind overflowed with fear. *How am I going to handle this?* I felt like a little girl, but I knew I wasn't. Suddenly... a memory of a feeling, just for a second or two.

It was me... feeling and knowing my pregnancy. Warmth... careful... motherhood. Sometimes, I could hear a faint lullaby in my mind. Then, it vanished... and so did the thought.

I recall thinking "how silly" the testing was as Diane proceeded. I remember *feeling* just the same as before. I wasn't at all cognizant of what exactly "took place." I didn't want to make a big deal about why I was hospitalized, or what had happened. Now, with the notebook as my memory, it became evident I had literally no short term recollection. It was pretty unnerving, too. The thing was, I couldn't remember that it was unnerving. I just didn't want to be regarded as an albatross around the neck.

Unresolved experiences came back with *vengeance*. Moments in my life when I was struck with fear. My brain brought back anything that I had tucked away in the recesses of my mind, never wanting to divulge for the pain caused... and it was constant. The specific moments of indecision were strong and caused the most damage in my development as a human being. I clearly could see the consequence of mistakes I had made, and how they had harmed me. I was witnessing my life as a *critique*... and I was not able to stop. It was like MGM's *"The Ten Commandments,"* with Charleton Heston, but it was *me* instead. My life clarified with

60

intensity. For the first time, I was precisely able to be objective about situations I had been confronted with in my life. In my past, I had been unable to see the forest through the trees, but now I knew exactly how I should have responded. Now, I knew how I should have handled myself, but it was too late. It is the past. From what I could see as my mind relentlessly spewed out this information, it was not anything *I* had done, but what I had been confronted with during my life. It was, what others had done to *me*. I could clearly see, my innocence was damaging, like a fawn to the wolves. *Why didn't I know any better? Why didn't I see the danger in that?*

My right side was extremely swollen, from trauma and lack of circulation. Surprisingly, I didn't give it much thought... as there were so few thought to give. There were only memories. I know that I had the mind of a child because I remember it. I feel very protective of the child who I was.

~ ~ ~ ~ ~ ~

After the first week of placement testing, Chris handed me a pair of eyeglasses and told me they were mine. I vehemently denied they were .

"I.............. don't............ wear............. glasses!
.........I've................. *never*......... worn........... glasses!"

Chris suggested I try them on, and explained I had worn contact lenses for years. Within a few seconds after trying them on, I lowered my head, as I took in the memories of my life with my glasses.

Gladwyne Elementary School, *First grade... crying... little blue horn-rimmed glasses with a patch. Sixth grade, terrorized for ugliness. Ninth grade, "ugly-four-eyed-bitch..."*

How could I forget my glasses? I had *forgotten who I was...* Now, I thought of them as an old friend rather than something contrite. They spoke of me, and my imperfections... and my longing to be *faultless*. I wondered why didn't I see the damage those thoughts had caused me. Now, it was so clear.

Chris wheeled me down to a spacious room with mirrors, exercise machines and low padded tables. I met "Adam". He began some kind of evaluation. Then, he left to answer a telephone call. After a while, he returned and in an enthusiastic voice said, "Madeleine Hopkins!"

Madeleine... Madeleine Hopkins... that's me! Gosh, that's me! Hopkins is **my** *name! I am married to Chris...*

On February 13, Chris asked me if I would like to take some time to get a card for Valentine's Day. I didn't seem to care about it, but somehow, I knew that I had *always been* one who cared. We took the elevator down to the first floor of the hospital where there was a small store. Chris told me he would leave the immediate area so that I would be able to select a card. After a few minutes standing at the cards, I was not able to determine what I was supposed to do. I tried to gather my wits before Chris knew I was having a problem, but I couldn't. I walked over to him, feeling very foolish and asked what type of card I was supposed to buy. There were so many, and each one was directed at a particular relationship. There were cards from *"Honey,"* cards to *"My Wife,"* and cards to the *"One I love,"* but my mind was not able to categorize. I was not able to put myself on the receiving end so that I would be able to select a card accordingly. It was too confusing. I was completely disconcerted and quietly broke down in the store. Everything was wrong in my mind. I was shocked and despondent.

~ ~ ~ ~ ~ ~

Several times since I had come to the Rehab floor, I had seen the man whom I remembered from before I had *come down to Earth*. I had specific "flashbacks" of certain people, and I realized my memory had attempted to function at certain points in time. But one man in particular, stayed in my mind. Finally, I was able to surmise, this man was the connection. He was why I was here... wherever I was. I forced myself to ask questions concerning "the man" in very limited way, and reality started to take form.

He's the one. He's the reason I'm here. Did he help me? What is wrong with me? What did he do for me?

I felt a connection with him, but I didn't know why. He always lead the way through the corridors in the hospital... *leader of the pack*. But, I couldn't organize my thoughts in order to ask the specific questions. One day, I tapped on my leg to get Chris's attention. Chris looked at me and I indicated the need to know who the man was.

"His name is Doctor Kotapka."

Of course... he's a doctor. Doctor Kotapka. That's the name I keep hearing.

I was afraid to ask any more than that. Although, in the silence of my thoughts, I began to explore the possibilities and I was frightened.

*What is it that he **does?***

In my efforts to function, it never occurred to me to ask Chris... or maybe I was afraid to ask.

I was unable to say his name. I tried over and over in the privacy of my room only to find that when confronted with the simple task, I was absolutely *tongue-tied*. There was a *consonant cluster* right in the middle, so that each time I tried, I was not able to *enunciate* his name. As a result, there was silence. Every time I saw him coming through the halls, once or twice weekly, I had an overwhelming desire to express my endless gratitude, (for what, I didn't exactly know) ... but, never did. I knew that his life was filled with poor souls like me, and I felt that it would be most inappropriate. Although, in my mind, the event took place one thousand times.

~ ~ ~ ~ ~ ~

During the first week in rehab, my occupational therapist Christine Motisko, asked me with which hand I wrote. Immediately, I had a memory of a meeting with a man. *Who is this person?* I let the memory play itself out and realized the scene was a doctor's office. *Where am I?* Within seconds I started to get my bearings, but my short-term memory deficit made it totally impossible to function logically. I couldn't *remember* that I had a short-term memory problem *because* of the short-term memory problem, but every once in a while a memory would stick.

In the flashback, the doctor was telling me to use my left hand to relieve my right hand of *over-use syndrome*. Now, I was told the opposite. I was to use my right hand for everything. The two conflicting messages in my brain were constantly causing a problem for me. A number of times I attempted to communicate this to the therapists, but it was too much for my brain to find the route from the *thought to the articulation.* Then, within seconds, what I had just been thinking, was gone. I wanted more than anything to have a conversation with someone without a loss of words. I knew what I wanted to say from one minute to the next, but there were so few words from my mouth. All the therapists spoke to me as if I were hard-of-hearing in an effort to make clear the incoming message. That just about drove me crazy but how could they have known? I couldn't write it down, and I never thought about using a computer or typewriter which might have made a difference; it's hard to say. I had seen a movie about a man who had severe physical and communication deficits *(My Left Foot)*. He eventually found a way to let people be aware that he was a mentally functioning human being capable of loving, hating, feeling frustrated, being happy or sad. Now, in a way I was in his shoes.

It was a sad time: I cried *a lot* remembering fragments of my life. I kept thinking I would be back to normal in a week... then a week would pass, and I'd think maybe another week...

~ ~ ~ ~ ~ ~

The entire time I was at HUP, I was well aware of the fact that I was being watched. Not just by the nurses, but also the interns. They would "make the rounds" at 5:30 A.M., like clockwork. I was desperately trying to become cognizant, and tried to keep a sunny disposition... even at 5:30 A.M.. I specifically recall the feeling of being under the microscope as the interns looked down on me as if I were a science project. The thing is... I was. I felt as if I didn't exist. I remember thinking, *I am a person, just like you. Don't disregard me; I am important too.* At the beginning, I was unaware of my appearance: half shaved head and eight months pregnant. I guess I would've stared too. After a while, I became uncomfortable with the fact I had almost no privacy, but I also knew there was not much that could be done about it.

There was one intern who did more than briefly stare. This one actually observed my actions as if he knew there was a person under there. I held his stare for a while. *Do you see me?* I thought. *Do you see that I'm more than what you see?*

Sometimes, strangers would come into my room just to stare at me. Perhaps, to see my reaction. Perhaps, just to see... and I hated that. I was a person, not a freak and I had feelings. Chris never allowed such invasions, but he was not able to be there all the time. I began to dread moments of his departure.

Many times during naps after lunch, or after therapy in the late afternoon, I would be awakened by a nurse or even Chris, and be so alarmed I would cry out, as one does from a nightmare. It was a startle reflex that would shock me profoundly. My heart would pump furiously for a couple of minutes while I tried desperately to pull myself together.

The feeling of *impending doom* could not be abolished. I recognized it as the same internal wrenching that I experienced when my first husband was killed... but it was different. It was more intense because there were no breaks. His death affected me in *waves* but this was *constant*, like being *completely* under water. Drowning every second. My mind was spinning, and spinning. My body was unstable, I felt unsure and infirm. Constantly, I focused on fixed objects in an effort to balance myself while standing. The lack of feeling on my right side, coupled with the pregnancy caused my gait to be unstable and wide. In my mind, my hips were very far apart.

During the weeks on the rehab floor, I thought everyone had the same problem as me. I wasn't able to comprehend the individual medical problems of each person. It was too complex for my mind. At one point, an unruly patient looked at me with a sneer and blurted, "What's wrong with you?"

It didn't occur to the woman that my half shaved head was an indication of a recent brain trauma? Why should it occur to her? It certainly didn't occur to me that I needed to point that out to her! Even in the rehab it was still a "dog-eat-dog-world". I couldn't get the words out to explain my condition. I couldn't even formulate the words in my mind. I felt useless and defeated... and angry.

"Today we finished some more testing...
Madeline became briefly tearful."

Diane Kendall

The discussions about *aphasia* were a problem for me. I had never heard of aphasia before, and was confused about what it was and suddenly, it had become a major part of my life.

If I focused intensely, I was somewhat able to absorb information. Short-term recall was the major problem and the fact that I couldn't place myself in time relative to my life. I remember working with Diane, trying to respond to cards she would hold up depicting the most fundamental things. *Tree... fork... lamp... umbrella etc...* I recognized the items but was unable to label them. Very basic, *simple* words, with very basic, uncomplicated meanings. My ability to *form words* had been eradicated.

Diane would ask what I did for a living, or what I did in my spare time. I recall not quite knowing the answer. It was all so complex... and I couldn't explain, because I could not quite remember. I didn't have anything to show for myself. I didn't remember to ask Chris where my pocketbook was either, which would have my wallet. The wallet had my business card and my "Seller's Certificate" for my gallery. Still, it might have been too difficult to explain, or retract. There was always an unspoken identity within me. Perhaps, that was my soul. It was strong and constant and whatever it was, it held me together.

I thought a lot about God, hoping God was protecting me. I had never quite understood God, all my life it had escaped me. *Always*, I sought to understand the complexities of true faith... but now, every day, *every hour*, time moved so slowly and I wished that I could have the knowledge of a greater power to pull me through.

~ ~ ~ ~ ~ ~

3

Impact

    I couldn't comprehend the severity of my situation. Diane tried many times to explain why I was there, and the result of "the bleed." I could not understand why I couldn't write or talk. I knew there was an alphabet but I couldn't recite the letters of the alphabet. I knew there was a numerical system but I couldn't remember the order of numbers. I knew my name was Madeleine but I couldn't spell it. I felt totally useless, and unbelievably scared. Everything I did was wrong. She spelled my name out on paper and I saw that she had spelled it incorrectly. I shook my head from side to side. She handed me the pen and I was able to make an "e" after the "l" (Madeleine).

    "*This* is how you spell your name?" she asked. I nodded.

    "I'll have to check with Chris," she said.

    Doesn't she see me? Doesn't she see how hard this is? How hard I'm trying? What will it take for people to understand? Something has happened to me!!!

    The next session was more of the same. Once again, I broke down in my frustration of *not knowing*.

    Diane wrote out, *I see with my* _____ , but I was unable to "fill in the blank." I tried to communicate the fact that I needed to know what had happened, and she drew an image of a face with a line down the center. She wrote *Left* on one side of the face and then she made an asterisk and told me something happened on the left side. Suddenly, *I realized.*

"I........... had......... a... **stroke?!**   I... had a **stroke?**".

Diane nodded and seemed puzzled at my reaction. How was I to know? No one had told me.

I sat searching for a response, a revelation perhaps, but I was *simply aghast.* Everyone had been referring to my condition as if it was nothing of significance, probably in an effort to cushion the impact... but the cushioning only served it's purpose to those without the reasoning problems!   I'd never heard of the term "bleed." In my state of mind, I did not realize people were referring to my brain. The awareness level had not been reached yet, although I knew something was terribly wrong. To suddenly realize what happened could be classified as a stroke made more sense that anything *anyone* had said, especially because of my severe comprehension deficits.

No wonder I can't talk! *No wonder* I can't remember anything! So *this* is the problem! Why didn't anyone tell me? *Why?*

Within minutes, I already lost sight of the impact. Yet, in my notebook which I carried with at all times, was the diagram Diane had just drawn. I couldn't juggle this information and retain it at the same time. I left her office with a few pieces of the puzzle missing and off I went.

I was furious with Chris and that was one memory that stuck. Then, I would forget what I was angry about, and I would go back in time again, step-by-step... until I found the source of the anger. It didn't matter that Chris was instructed *not* to say anything to me for fear of a negative response. It was me.

He should have told me.

He should have told me.

He should have told me.

In a few days, the only memory I had of that session with Diane was the fact that my problem was stroke. But, I couldn't remember exactly what stroke was. It pained me to ask Chris. Everything in my brain was so scrambled, I simply couldn't remember.

Is it my heart?

Is it my leg?

Is it my hand?

70

I had to ask him what part of the body is affected by a stroke. Chris looked at me square in the eye, and said "The brain." I thought of Diane's drawing.

*Oh no... oh no... **My brain**. Of course... That's what is wrong. How could I have forgotten? Wait a second! That **is** why I forgot! **It's my brain! It's me!!!***

My memory was flooded with information about the impact of a brain injury, and how devastating they are. My mind pulled out every single bit of stored knowledge whether it was from textbooks or from family history. Each retrieval of information was no less devastating than that before it. I remembered my parents stressing the importance of protecting my head because once the damage is done nothing is ever the same.

I tried to appear self-confident by not asking too many questions, but more often that not, it backfired, and I would once again suffer the humility. The bleed robbed every aspect of my being, it showed no mercy.

I needed to know what was left from the bleed and it was Diane's job to make it known. I don't believe I gave much thought to the fact that I was right-handed but I knew I was an artist. Like water, and air, and earth... my soul was clearly defined. Without a doubt, I understood that was, who I was. I recall Diane asking me *"What do you do for a living?"* and I was unable to say *I an artist* because I didn't know the word for artist, yet I knew that was who I was.

Mostly, I thought about my past but not by choice, my mind was spewing out memory after memory with no relation. It just kept coming... and coming... and coming. Every five seconds, another *isolated* flashback would come to mind leaving no trace of the *preceding* flashback. Memories of every *person, place or trauma* I had experienced in my life and with each memory came the intense emotions that I had experienced at that time in my life. I couldn't make it stop, whether it was the memory of my first friendships or moments of glory or trauma, it was all there with unrelenting and unforeseen clarity.

I began to receive *"get well"* cards, and with each card I retracted moments in time with each person (or persons) who sent the card. My recollections revealed times, places and faces from my past and not one of the letters or cards was taken for granted. Each

71

one was like gold: sparkling and shimmering in the recesses of my mind. I only wish I could have responded.

I received a card from the contractor I had been working with in York, Maine. A memory, undiminished. In a second, I visualized all of the design jobs that were associated with that contractor.

The dentist's office, with a play area for children...
The house by the sea with the curved stair... the foyer with the cathedral ceiling...

Like a tidalwave in my mind, suddenly there were huge pieces of my life trying to make their way in a sea of time, and places and moments. Another card from the owners of a restaurant I redesigned, and once again, a rush of memory.

"Why aren't you doing this for a living?"
"Well, I was. I moved up here because I was hired for a
position in an architectural firm in Portsmouth, but I
lost my job."
"Why did you lose the job?"
"Well, I don't really know, they never told me."
"They never gave you a reason?"
"No... they never gave me a reason. I didn't see the point
in fighting for the job if they didn't want me. I went
through something similar a couple times before. I just
figured it was me... that's why I was waiting tables."
"Wow. You know, you should get back into it."
"I know... I will. I just need to get my bearings."

I tried to place architectural design jobs in time. They all seemed so long ago, but again, I kept realizing that I was able to retrieve these memories like gathering precious diamonds from a mine deep in the earth.

I received pieces of my life through the mail, mostly from Maine. A letter from the home-owners of a re-design I had done, including photos of the property and their children.

72

They did the *renovation that I designed...*

I looked at their children, they looked as if they were the same age as when I did the design work. Suddenly, I realized these jobs I had done must not have been ten years ago, they were recent. Very recent. My sense of time was entirely out or order. No sooner did I realize this, I forgot about it... until the next time I looked at the photographs.

Lorraine Fisher, my boss at Kenneth Parker Associates, in Philadelphia, sent a card... and Kenneth, too.

***I was working** at KPA, in Philadelphia, when Doug lost his life. So painful... so sad. Oh no... not this. I can't go there again... I don't want to go there again!*

Flashbacks of suffering I had suppressed. Now, it was there with the same intensity, as though it had just happened. But I couldn't make it stop. It dragged me down to a place where nightmares are kept.

Everyday, *every minute,* I tried to place myself in time. I received cards from relatives, both distant and close. At the same time, I felt embarrassed that they knew about my condition... *everyone knew.* Juxtaposing my life at HUP with my former life was too much to bear, yet it was all I did.

One of the cards was from a Portsmouth architectural firm where I had worked, but I was unable to place the time. More than that, it was an unpleasant departure.

***I was called** into a small conference room. In three days, I would be flying to London for vacation. I wondered what he wanted to ask me? It had been over two months since the last "talk".*

"Before you go, I'll need your resignation."

"Do you mean a temporary leave of absence for my trip?" I said.

"No, I mean, I will need a formal letter of resignation."

"But, I'm not resigning."

"Well, it's either that, or I could fire you, which would ruin your chances of ever finding a decent job."

Now... *why* would they send me a card? I needed the card when I was completely shattered! I didn't understand the motive. I was puzzled because I remembered fragments of losing my job, but the perplexity of the scene was too much, or maybe the puzzlement had always been the problem. There were faces from my past before my eyes. I realized the main issue now, was I *remembered*. The memory was intact, albeit a painful one, it was there. I dusted it off and tried to let it be, but it wouldn't take it's place in the cobwebs of my memory. It just hung there, black widow that it was. Unresolved.

~ ~ ~ ~ ~ ~

Christine, the occupational therapist, provided me with a special fork that was padded for gripping as there was no feeling or strength in my right side. I resented what the fork represented: the loss of function in my right hand. I hated the fact that I couldn't feel my fingers. Just as a surgeon... or a musician would react with the loss of their digits, my fingers were my life. My hand was lifeless and unrecognizable. Even the nails were foreign. I cradled my hand and cried for it. The loss was *overwhelming*.

In physical therapy one day, a handful of doctors approached me. They greeted me by name and asked me to perform a few functions. They asked me to wiggle the fingers of my right hand, so I did. They were exhilarated.
"Madeleine, could you grab this pencil?" one said.
I grabbed the pencil with my left hand.
"Can you use your right hand Madeleine?"
I looked at my right hand, which I couldn't *feel*. Silently, told it to move and watched it grab the pencil. Based on their reactions, you would have thought I had just walked on the moon. I guess I had. They knew about my condition; they knew I'd been in a coma; they'd seen everything.

74

Privacy was rare on rehab, there were always interruptions whether it be time for pills, a BP check or an overview of the patient's condition. One Sunday afternoon, I was watching the television in my room. The TV had become a learning tool. Watching people interact in commercials, on sitcoms, etc. gave me clues about how I might relate to people. It also told me how different I had become, as I was not the least bit interested in the dialogue of a talk show or the theme of a story. It disturbed me intensely.

There was a knock on my door. *"Yes?"*

The door opened and there was one of the therapists, but not one I had been working with.

"May I come in?" she asked.

"Okay" I said.

I thought she wanted to talk about something, but she proceeded to open a book and start reading. I was trying to assess the situation but with each second that passed, I found myself becoming less comfortable. I didn't have the luxury of insight. Finally, I couldn't take it any longer, so I wheeled myself out of my room. I never found out why she came to see me. Did she think I was incapable of understanding?

Mom

There's that lady again.

She told me who she was,
But I can't remember.

I think she is someone important.

I think she is someone I should know,
But, I can't recall.

I just can't remember.

As I drifted off to sleep one night, I had a serge of recollection of the moment I had woken from the coma.

A woman was there when I woke, but I seemed to drift in and out of who she was... mostly out. There, next to the bed was a table with a telephone. The woman made a phone call and put my ear to the receiver. I was having trouble with the concept of a telephone... what was I supposed to do with it? Suddenly, a man's voice came through the receiver. It was a familiar voice... friendly, so I knew it must have been someone I knew but I was too embarrassed to admit that I couldn't place the voice.

The voice said, "Hi! How are you feeling?"

"Okay...," I said.

"I'm sorry that I'm not with you, but I'll see you tomorrow, okay?"

"Okay," I replied. It didn't seem to matter that I had just spoken with someone whose voice was unfamiliar, because with seconds I had forgotten anyway. I wondered who this woman was, too. She was very quiet, soft-spoken but... she was fussing with me. I felt a need to say something, but I didn't know what I wanted to say.

The woman was leaving, when suddenly the word "Mom" came out of my mouth.

The relationship with my mother was one of the most distressing aspects of the life I had "awakened into." Our relationship had always been significant to me and was important to our family as a whole. But now, I didn't really care; there didn't seem to be a point to it. There didn't seem to be a bond with her as there had been before the bleed. She was a stranger to me.

At some point early on, Mom asked me if I remembered that Leslie, my sister, had died. We didn't talk about the period of time surrounding her death, only that she was gone. I nodded, but I resented that she had asked. It was so private, deeply painful and personal and it was a part of me that nobody was allowed to see. Especially, someone who I didn't know... or remember. At the same time, I remembered my mother and my relationship with her in the past. Now, there didn't seem to be a connection in the heart, or in

78

the mind... and it was sad. Within seconds, details of the thought, and the thought itself, was gone.

Soon after, I realized the same had happened to one of my brothers... a lost bond. I began to realize my *own* importance in my family. I could see myself clearly *missing* from my kindred. The effort to regain my position in the *soul* of the family, was another priority in my mind. It was a matter of deduction.

My Mother came with me to get my hair cut one day. As I sat in the chair looking at my reflection in the mirror, I became despondent.   Just for a moment, suddenly I could see the devastation before me. I saw a glimpse of who I had been, I felt a piece of the *me* I had been. Immediately, I broke down. I could not believe this was me.

"What is it, Dear?," Mom said.

I couldn't get words out in addition to a complete loss of emotional control.

"Oh, *Dear*... it took you so long to grow it, didn't it?!"

It wasn't the hair!!! *It was the mess of a human being staring back at me!!!* The hairdresser suggested the look was the current style. Mom chimed in on the suggestion that I keep the *"half-head look,"* which is always convenient when faced with indecisiveness.

One day, I tried to put some make-up on but the order of application was *all wrong*. It wasn't just that, I couldn't remember how much to put on or... not put on. Diane was with me, watching and I was too embarrassed to admit that I couldn't remember how. I kept trying to make it right. Everything I did was backwards.

I would take up to ten minutes to fasten my watch, all the while Chris would remain silent as I was ever determined to do the simple task on my own. I was unable to tie my shoes as well and was given "shoe-buttons." Even so, it would take five minutes to work my fingers.

Everyday, I took pills: *many* pills: Phenobarbital, vitamins, iron, Tylenol, and more. Chris questioned the long term effects the Phenobarbital may have on the child within me. I was so wrapped up in my own problems with reality, that I simply didn't remember the fact that I was pregnant. I felt ashamed of my self-centeredness. There was a baby inside me but all I thought about was me... I couldn't help it. It was the way it was. It was my mind at the age of eight years old.

Brass Ring

On a carousel,
　　　Going around, and around
　　　　　and around.
　　　　　　　Very fast, too fast...
　　　　　　　　　Can't grab that brass... ri-i-i-i-i-ng!

Oh... There! I got it!
　　　*Put it over there, in a **safe** place.*
　　　　　Let me steady myself. Gosh!
　　　　　　　Is it supposed to go so... fa-a-a-ast?

Hold on, here it comes again!
　　　Got it! Did you see?
　　　　　I got it again!
　　　　　　　Just need to rest a... whi-i-i-i-ile.

I can't?
　　　*But, I'm so tired... **so** tired...*
　　　　　And I don't want to sleep,
　　　　　　　For then, it will be a new... da-a-a-a-ay...

In preparation of the upcoming birth of the child within me, Diane asked me to sing *"Happy Birthday."* I tried, only... I couldn't. The *tune* was right but the *words* were *not*. It was a bizarre, puzzling moment as my mind could not cooperate with a command. All that came out was, *"Ter pde sekt eob kxs, Mensa brems tnxz ..."* No recognizable *words but* the "Happy Birthday" melody was intact. It was the same strange impact that is found when helium is inhaled and a voice changes only in this case, the *words* changed. Both of us laughed, but my thoughts were far from merriment. I was alarmed. Everything I did was so wrong. Every word, every action... only my thoughts were genuine.

If I mentioned a pain in my abdomen, Chris would ask what exercises I might have done to aggravate my system. Then he asked if it was hunger, as usual I could never remember when I ate... and *not ever* remembered that I was "eating-for-two." The only way I knew I had brushed my teeth, was if my toothbrush was wet. I had no appetite. There was no way of knowing whether my bladder was full. The same was true of my bowels. Slowly, I learned new ways of reading my body... in a *deductive* way.   Because of the damage to my brain, everything I did was reversed. I tried to compensate, but I couldn't. Because of the short-term memory loss, bodily discomforts indicated needs. I couldn't feel anything on my right side, and my brain was sending confused signals to my left side.

~ ~ ~ ~ ~ ~

I began remembering bits of information about my life, but I couldn't place the "where" or the "when" of things. I couldn't grasp time in relation to my life. All memories were floating around in my mind but I wasn't able to put those memories in any kind of order. Abstract thoughts were running amock. The concept of time was irrelevant. I couldn't stop it, but I began trying to piece bits of information together.

I was an artist.

I had an architectural design business.

I graduated from RISD in 1982.

They were milestones in my life, which I desperately seemed to need. Validation.

Vague memories began coming into my mind, of seeing doctors about tingling and numbing on my right side, but I couldn't quite remember when I had seen them. In addition, the memories were *floating*, not fixed. As much as I tried, I was not able to stop the constant flow, like a turbulent river... only moving in one direction.

I remembered seeing a social worker, but I couldn't recall *why*. It seemed like it had happened ten years ago, then in the middle of thinking about it... the thought would be gone, again. Because I couldn't write, I simply *thought* about everything, including who I was. Because of the short term memory loss, I didn't remember to talk about it with the therapists. Sometimes I would try but the concepts were too complex to convey. My mind was like a carousel and I kept losing the *"brass ring."* I couldn't reach the brass ring... and the *brass ring* was my thoughts... my memories.

There was an inability to differentiate between thoughts and actions. I *thought* I had done something, but I hadn't at all. Like dreaming while awake. I didn't want it to happen any longer and it concerned me. I could see how this condition could be hazardous.

My right side was completely numb, like nothing... like air. I guarded it, especially my hand and arm. I didn't want anything to happen to it. I thought of it as a wounded animal needing warmth and care. It didn't feel like it was attached to my body at all... so I would watch them to make sure they were exactly where I *thought* they were. Many times, *"in my mind's eye"* my hand would be gripping something or in a certain position only to find that it was limp and hanging... lifeless. I began to see why PT and OT are so important in rehab: to keep the damaged areas of the brain stimulated so that eventually... hopefully, the brain will re-route, taking detours around areas that have been damaged.

Chris kept his hand on the pulse of my life. He was with me always. He slept on the floor of my room. He was my friend; he knew there was nothing else that he could be... he knew that I was not able to be anything more.

~ ~ ~ ~ ~ ~

It's gone ... *it's just... gone. Isn't it?* I said to
myself. I lowered my head. *My mind is
gone.*
"Why are you crying?" ...but, no words came.

~ ~ ~ ~ ~ ~

I asked Chris to gauge my recovery. Phrasing the question alone took a few minutes as the speech center of my brain was the most damaged by the bleed.

"How..... bad... is... it?" I asked.

Chris hesitated. "It's hard to determine. Each area of *you*, has been affected."

I tried to organize the words in my mind. I wanted to know the extent of the damage, but could not use words. I felt panic and dread and desperation. There must be a way of relating the question.

"On............ a............ per-r-rcen-n-ntage. One........... hundred.......... percent...........was........... me........... then. What......... am........... I.............. now."

Chris deliberated.

"What............ percen-t-t-tage.............. of.......... my....... mind............ of.......... my........... being........... is............. *there?"*

Chris paused, and said, "Thirty percent."

I thought he hadn't understood the question, so I began again.

"I understand what you're asking. You're thirty percent of who you were."

I searched his eyes for an indication of a miscommunication. His expression was of a grave and solemn nature. I felt sick to my stomach. How could it be that so much was gone? *Where has it gone*, I wondered... and *will I get it back?* I was devastated by his words. The floor had fallen from beneath my feet and from that day on, I asked Chris every few days, then every few weeks about my recovery. I wanted everything back... or as much as I could possibly *get* back.

Every time I took a nap, when I woke, I thought it was a new day. I was taking two naps a day for the pregnancy but also for the AVM bleed recovery. Throw in the fact that I never knew the day to begin with and you've got yourself one frustrated individual.

For a while, there was something blocking my sight but I couldn't remember to say anything about it. Finally, I mentioned it to Chris. I could actually see it... but had difficulty describing it. It looked like a *hairball*, like thick, tangled hairs... *in my line of vision*.

I had an eye exam and it was determined whatever it was, would probably dissipate in time.

84

My physical therapist, Adam DeClerico, walked with me around the rehab floor everyday. At one point, he asked me if I could run. I had a flashback of running with my dog in Valley Forge park.

"Yes........ I.......... can.......... run..."

He asked me to demonstrate.

In my mind's eye, I knew exactly what jogging looked like, but when my body started moving, it didn't work. It felt like I had become the *Tin Man* in the movie *The Wizard of Oz*, as Dorothy found him rusted, and unable to move.

"If only I had my oil can," I thought.

If only I had a *brain*. At least, I remembered *The Tin Man*.

Deep Freeze

Silent memories rushing
Through a wounded mind.
Is this my life?
A fragment of memory?
Would help me find the rest?

The cold winter air brings
An endless flow of memories.
Painting by the ocean... the cold air...
Winter in Maine.

I close my eyes and remember.
Oh, I remember now.
There is my life... right there.

I can almost touch it.
Let me stay a while.

It is so clear.

Approaching the end of February, Adam asked me if I had a coat and took me outside. It was odd that I was so nervous about going out. I realized I'd be away from the security of the 6th floor... and my room. There was an extraordinary fear within me but I fought it. A fear of the unknown, like a child having a nightmare. An anxiousness... a knot in my stomach and my chest. I remember thinking, *Who **am** I? How did I use to react about something as simple as going outside?* I had become "The Cowardly Lion"... afraid of *everything*. I felt as if I couldn't deal with anything but I knew that Adam would not let me down. He was HUP, I knew I could trust him.

As we walked towards the exit doors, I saw dozens of people who knew nothing about what had happened to me. People who had places to go... and people to meet. I took it in and I remembered that I was once someone *just like them...* and I missed that. *I was so far from that.*

We left the building, and crossed the street. Adam had me do some coordination-reaction tests. He never said, "Okay, I am going to do some tests now". He simply had me respond to his directions, like a dog doing tricks. Then, we sat on a bench before going back in the building. I began remembering many times and places from Maine... home. First, it was the sensory familiarity: *cold winter air*. Then, it was the solitude and the silence. This sensory *deja-vous* was accompanied by a clarity that took away the fear for a moment. My body was suddenly filled with warmth. At that moment, life seemed so clear but only in an abstract sense... only an emotional sense... a *right-side-of-the-brain-sense*.

Brain Injury

Remembering to breathe.

Remembering to eat,
*   Remembering to shower,*
*   Remembering musical preferences.*

Remembering the hour of the day,
*   day of the week,*
*   week of the month,*
*   month of the year.*

Remembering a schedule.

Remembering friends.
*   Remembering relatives,*
*   Remembering birthdays,*

Remembering the pregnancy.

Remembering what happened.

Remembering life...

I felt desperate everyday. The anxiety never diminished, from the moment Chris woke me, until the next opportunity I had to sleep. If my sleep was disturbed, I would scream and crawl inside myself. Sleeping was the only chance I had to calmly heal, but I didn't know that. I only knew that Chris was on my side, he had to be... he just had to be.

I had memories of people and moments in time, but they seemed like someone else's memories. I wasn't familiar with some of the places or faces that would suddenly come into my thoughts. It was like I was in someone else's body. I began to realize I was having "out-of-body" incidents, but I couldn't exactly explain this to anyone because I couldn't find the words.

Somehow, I was able to dream. The mental images were recurring and all took place in the hospital. In one dream, my room was on a balcony overlooking the nurses station. Every night, because of the pregnancy, I would need to go to the bathroom. Chris would help me, as my body was unsteady and weak, especially the right side. In waking at that hour, I would try to get my bearings before I did anything. *Who am I? Where am I? How did I get here? etc...* I woke thinking I was elevated or on a balcony.

I was in a large house with a front porch and dreamt the nurses floated up to my room. The interior of the house had a curved stairway leading to the bedrooms. The front yard was very large with some trees, specifically a large maple tree. There was always snow in the yard and it was always peaceful. Basically, my dreams were a reflection of the views out the windows of HUP. I began to remember I had always been a dreamer and would have insightful dreams about my life and those in my life. But now, as soon as my head hit the pillow, I was out. I remembered sleeping on my side, but now I slept on my back. I noticed when I was awakened in the morning, I was in the same position. I hadn't moved all night. According to Chris, *time* was on my side.

Chris always helped me and never complained about the hour or the inconvenience of sleeping on the floor of my room. At one point, he had to take care of some business in Maine and would be away for 3 days driving to Maine and back. The thought of his absence was frightening. I just couldn't control my emotions; I was embarrassed. I knew the lack of control had everything to do with the bleed but no matter what, I couldn't get a handle on it. I simply could not stop *bawling my eyes out.* I knew the lack of control was a result of the bleed and knowing that, I would surely gain strength... but it never happened.

While he was away, my Mom and Dad took turns spending time with me: lunch time, dinner time and even during breaks in the afternoon. During lunch one day, a new patient on the rehab floor was eating as if he were an animal: eating with his hands, drooling, etc. I was watching him in alarm, as he walked over to the utility sink and began vomiting loudly. No one seemed to notice but me. I expressed my horror to my Dad, who seemed to be unaffected by the scene and continued eating, which only made me more repulsed. Seeing the man heaving into the sink, combined with watching my Dad eating was too much for my senses. Everything in my view was surreal... and delayed. I was busy trying to deal with the man vomiting, only to witness the next image of my Dad eating and the two images *combined* in my mind. At that, I wheeled myself out of the dining room, leaving my Dad *in the dust* while I tried to get the images out of my head. In an effort to get me to accept the reality of my needing to be at HUP, Dad tried to lighten-up the situation, but it was to no avail.

~ ~ ~ ~ ~ ~

During the beginning of March, there was a baby shower organized by the therapists on the rehab floor. I didn't have the heart or the capability to refuse the party. Chris, Diane and the rec-therapist had tried to figure out my feelings on *the party concept* but I didn't seem to have any foresight on it... until the minute I walked in the room where the festivities were to be held. There were friends, relatives and hospital staff in attendance. I was overwhelmed at the intensity of the moment as all eyes focused on me. I just wanted to crawl into a hole. I realized within the first five minutes that I had made an error in judgment. Still, it was very kind of everyone, especially one friend who came from the Berkshires.

My old friend was my housemate from Rhode Island School of Design. I could see based on her reactions to me how severely the bleed had affected me. I remember thinking, *Can't you see?? It's **me**!!!* I knew deep-down inside *I was there*. I thought she would be able to see it in my eyes that I understood everything

she was saying... but she was not able to see past my appearance and my altered speech. Rather than speak with me she spoke with Chris away from me... and that hurt very deeply. My presence disturbed her and it was obvious. It was very difficult because I didn't want people to see me this way. I tried with every ounce of dignity I could muster to make the appearance seem effortless. An hour and a half later, I resigned to my room. I was beyond exhaustion.

~ ~ ~ ~ ~ ~

A friend

I lost a friend today.
Someone I've known all my life.

She was okay,
She was an artist.

Perhaps, you knew her...
Her name was...
Oh, what was her name?

It was just on the tip of my tongue.

Oh well,
If I remember,
I'll let you know.

I believe
     fate smiled & destiny
     laughed as she came to my cradle
"know this child will be able"
     laughed as she came to my mother
"know this child will not suffer"
     laughed as my body she lifted
"know this child will be gifted
     with love, with patience
     and with faith
     she'll make her way"

Natalie Merchant

4

Life

An amniocentesis was done in the early part of March to determine if the baby was developed enough to be taken. It was a very painful procedure, only to reveal it would be at least another week. The second amnio was even worse... but revealed it was time for the C-section.

No amount of preparation could aid me through this time. Six weeks ago, I awoke from a *coma* thinking I was a child, only to find I had a life with a man I didn't remember and was pregnant with his child. I was terrified and in no way felt ready for this immediate responsibility at this point in my recovery. Most of the time I wouldn't even remember I was pregnant, until someone pointed it out. I felt I had to put up a false front to everyone, to show that I was thrilled with the day of the birth. But I was not thrilled, I was scared. I needed time to heal. There were dozens of people who were thrilled for me. I felt my indifference blend into the masses. I felt shamed and confused at my listlessness maybe because... that was one thing I *knew* I was not. I just knew it.

On March 25, 1993 early in the morning, my body was numbed from the waist down, a procedure termed, "block." After a while my bed was wheeled to another area. I began to feel nervous, which was unusual considering the amount of Phenobarbital in my system. After that, the procedure was pretty quick. Chris was right there with me, holding my hand when the baby was taken out of my body. I couldn't see the delivery as there was a blue sheet separating the birth from my line of vision.. My entire life I always thought of this moment... wondering how it would be. Yet, here I was, and it wasn't how it was *ever* supposed to be.

I could feel a change in my blood pressure and then, overwhelming fatigue. I felt like I was slipping away, and was expecting someone to say, *We're losing Madeleine, Doctor!* But, no one said it.

Then, a funny little sound from the other side of the blue sheet. With all that had happened to Chris and me, somehow knowing the baby was a little girl seemed so complete, like it was all part of the plan. The nurse brought the little baby over to me and there were two clear blue eyes looking right at me. A beautiful little person, *knowing* who I was. We looked at each other and I whispered, "Hello... little... one. You... made...... it." She was perfect.

Chris no longer slept on the floor in my room at HUP. He and Elizabeth stayed at my parents' apartment in Philadelphia. All of us knew the difficulties we faced, so we took the "one-day-at-a-time" approach. The apartment was in the *2400 Chestnut Street* near 30th Street Train Station, only five minutes from the hospital. The entire time I was living at HUP I couldn't place myself. I was not able to remember the plan of the city. I would look out my window on the sixth floor at HUP and nothing was as I recollected. I might as well be in California, because nothing looked familiar.

The first few days without Chris were difficult. Oh, I would see him and Elizabeth everyday, but not on an hourly basis as before. I didn't remember where I had been taken to recover from the birth. I thought I was in a completely different building, far away from the sixth floor at HUP. At times I thought I was in a different part of the city; I was completely disoriented. I was alone for the first time since the bleed and all I did was think about fragments of the life that I once had, and weep. I was unable to break out of the "depression," only submerge further. After two hours, one of the O.B. doctor's stopped by see me and she could plainly see the mess I was in.

The brain injury had taken my inner strength away. I was weak and lacked identity. The person that I *was*, was no longer there... but, I began to remember her. I wanted her back. She was feisty, determined, decisive and very independent. Yet, here was the same person, constantly trying to get a grip on this new reality. When I returned to the sixth floor, after five days recovering from the birth, I recognized my need to try to be more independent. I was faced with that anyway but also I was *realizing*, just as a child becoming an adult begins to see life in a new way. It was a crash course in growing up again complete with all the fears and trepidation.

Fortunately, my old room on the sixth floor was still vacant and I was able to move back in again. It was so good to see everybody again, and I continued my therapy as before. Philadelphia was coming out of winter.

~ ~ ~ ~ ~ ~

We're off to see the Wizard,
The wonderful Wizard of Oz.
We hear he is a Wiz of a Wiz
If ever a Wiz there was!
If ever a wonderful Wiz there was,
The Wizard of Oz is one because
Because, because, because, because, because...
Because of the wonderful things he does!
We're off to see the wizard,
The wonderful wizard of Oz!

(No consonant clusters!!!)

Sometimes, I was able to speak a complete sentence without hesitation, yet most of the time, although I had a complete thought in mind, I was not able to articulate. Then, by the time I was ready to speak my mind, I would forget. Finding sentences or songs that I was able to sing without hesitations gave me hope. I began to understand my speech deficiency and how I may be able to work around it. The bulk of my speech problems were rooted in the phenomena known as a *consonant cluster.* I was thrilled one afternoon, when I was able to recite *without hesitation,* an entire verse of *"We're Off to See the Wizard",* from *The Wizard of Oz!* There was no point in becoming bitter about my new reality, rather I had to make the best of it. Everyday, I was surrounded by people. Keeping my fears and anguish intact was not possible, but I tried.

I made dinner for Chris as part of my occupational therapy. There had been much improvement in two months of therapy. I had gone from little or no functions on my right side, to anywhere from 10 to 50 percent strength. Cognitively, there had been improvements as well... but at a "snail's crawl." It was April now and Chris informed me the fight to recover had brought me 60 percent back. Constantly, I had memories of my former self. I just kept thinking and remembering. Layer upon layer of my mind found it's place again.

I didn't seem to have any clues as to the financial implications of my rehabilitation. For that matter, I didn't seem to have concepts of *any* financial matters. I remembered being in my gallery working on the monthly sales totals... without a calculator, as usual.

That was me, I thought.

I asked Chris about the cost of my hospitalization. I did not have even the slightest inkling of how much the hospitalization was costing and it began to bother me.

Chris told me, "Focus on therapy, don't worry about finances," but I wanted to know.

"One............ hundred............... dollars?"

Chris looked me square in the eye, with disbelief.

"No, more than that," he said.

"Two............. hun-n-n-dred...? I............. need............ to............. know............. Please............... tell.............. me."

Chris knew that I was not going to let it go.

"At this point, it would be at least half-a-million-dollars... maybe more. I haven't thought about it yet. I haven't received a bill yet."

"Half.............. a.... million.............. dollars?"

I was perplexed. I couldn't comprehend the sum. I asked Chris to write it down on paper.

$$\textbf{\textit{\$500,000.00}}$$

I looked at the paper. *That,* I understood.

"*Holy............ Toledo............ How............... are............ we............. going............. to............. pay............... for............. this?*"

"That's what we have insurance for honey. Don't think about it okay?"

Easy for him to say, I thought. He could see the bewildered look on my face, I felt hopeless and scared.

(In)dependence

Don't leave me alone!
(Leave me alone!)

Don't leave me!
(Leave me!)

Don't leave!
(Leave!)

(Don't leave me...)

5

Different Eyes

On April 1 1993, Adam gave me the "thumbs-up" for independent walking... no more wheelchair. You can't imagine what the feeling is like unless you are in one all the time... like a thousand butterflies lifted me out of the wheelchair beckoning me to fly with them. It was a wonderful feeling! That day and everyday I used a cane to walk. I was one of the lucky one's in this world.

I had become aware of my appearance and suddenly I felt self-conscious. It was time to join civilization again.

Every once in a while, I would come close to the mind I remembered. At the end of the day before I went to sleep, Chris and I would have a moment or two to think and talk. Suddenly, I would become quite *lucid*. My speech deficit would be non-existent and I would become very level-headed.

Christine took several patients from the rehab floor to the *Reading Terminal Market*, a farmers-style-market in the heart of the city complete with restaurants, deli's and food counters. Visually and cognitively it was an overload to my system but it felt *so good* to be there. In the same block was the American Restaurant Association (ARA) building. I had worked on the ARA building for *Kenneth Parker Associates, Corporate Interiors*, just prior to my move to Maine. I thought about my *"ARA days"* the entire day and months after too, like a bizarre dream of faces and moments in time. The images out of my past appeared, and suddenly I would remember names, places and moments of times long gone.

The impact of being out in the city was alarming. At once, I saw all of the difficulties I would face in the years ahead. My delayed reactions both physically and cognitively; even something as simple as walking. Every nerve focused on the walk itself... the destination, the breathing, talking while walking... things that are taken for granted by all of us. I had to make it all look effortless.

A few days later Christine took me to a large grocery store. I had a list of items that I was to purchase but I couldn't focus. I would completely miss items that I was looking for even though the item would be right smack in view. This problem was not only in the grocery store but *everywhere*.

Christine was talking loudly not realizing she was drawing attention to herself. I became embarrassed and reluctantly asked her to "keep-it-down." The whole situation was bad enough without drawing attention to it.

I started to feel that things were going to be all right, as long as I kept focused. I had been working on my independence, because I needed to prove to the therapists, to Chris... and to myself that I *could* be independent. I had been doing everything towards that goal: waking, showering, dressing and continuing my rehab therapy.

Four times a day, I nursed Elizabeth, although the pressure to give-up nursing was always a topic of controversy. I didn't understand why there was the urgency to begin with. All I had to give of myself to Elizabeth, was what Mother Nature had provided. There was absolutely no way that it was going to be any other way. Suddenly, there was clarity and it was for my child.

Don't they know about the bond? Don't they realize that this is what life is? Please! Don't make me lose the bond with my child!

Everything about who I was had been taken from me: my freedom, my independence and my capabilities. But now, I had to make certain that I play by "their" rules, or risk losing the maternal bond with my child. I began feeling panic at the possibility of losing Elizabeth due to my condition. *Everything that I did* took three-times-longer than before, because of delays in my thought process.

104

There were times when I was five or ten minutes late to therapy and I knew that it would be documented.

One day, I was determined *not* to be late. The morning nurse woke me at 5:45 AM. I washed-up, dressed and put my shoes on (which in itself was a five minute endeavor), and walked down to the dining room. I wanted Diane to see that I could do it... and I did it. I was outside her office with five minutes to spare. After fifteen minutes, she still hadn't come. A janitor came by, asking if I needed help.

"No.......... I'm.......... just.......... waiting.......... for.......... Diane," I said.

The janitor pointed out that it was Saturday, there was no therapy today. So much for keeping focused.

~ ~ ~ ~ ~ ~

Diane organized a meeting with the patients to discuss the various medical conditions of those on the rehab floor. One by one, each person spoke of the intensity of their malady. It was the first time I had learned of all the different medical ailments of anyone on rehab. I empathized with each person, and I was having great difficulty keeping my emotions intact. I felt as if I heard one more heart wrenching story I may not be able to contain myself. I knew I couldn't speak although I really wanted to.

When it was my turn, I couldn't get my words out. I looked over at Diane and she said something about my illness, something that I had never heard from anyone. Then, she turned it over to me... and I wasn't prepared. I couldn't formulate any words, they just wouldn't come out. I lost control of my emotions again in front of the whole crowd, which only exacerbated the situation. Diane suggested moving on to the next patient, but I wanted so much to tell my story. I wanted them to know that I *had* a good life! I wanted them to know that I was originally from this area, but now lived in Maine! I wanted them to know that I have a husband named Chris and a new baby... Elizabeth! I wanted them to know all these things I had just found out about *me*!

As I choked back my tears, all that I could say was, *"All.............................. of.............................. you.....................
have.......................... been.............................. through...................*

105

so.................................... much."

There was silence. *That* in itself, took about a minute to utter. In my mind, I had nothing to complain about. For some reason, I had a feeling everything was going to be okay, down the road. I looked at all of them. I didn't want to cry, but I couldn't stop the outpouring of emotion. I felt like a fool, an imbecile. I wanted them to know who I was, but I couldn't. All the people in the room were dealing with physical traumas, all of which would leave them with disabilities for the rest of their lives. I was sitting there with my new haircut and mascara on my eyelashes and felt that I had nothing to complain about. I wasn't able to put anything in perspective for the people in the group. It was too much for my mind to handle. There was so much of a loss for me to try to explain to these strangers and with my inability to communicate, it all remained stuck inside.

At the next session, Diane wanted to see how I would perform with daily activities. I had *rehearsed* everyday functions with her in her office, but now... it was *show time*. We left the building and went to the post office, only a few doors away. Then, the bank. The entire time, I *had* to be intensely focused, or I would lose my train of thought, or purpose of being. We went into a MacDonald's restaurant, I ordered french fries and a drink. I couldn't taste it, but that wasn't the point. The point was, my ability to function and remain centered. I was well aware of the resistance in my mind, like a huge boulder in my path. Such simple tasks, and I knew that... but it was unbelievably strenuous, internally. We left the restaurant, and were headed back to HUP when Diane suggested we sit on a bench before going back inside.

"Okay," I said.

Everything in this new life had a goal attached... I didn't know anything else. Diane sat, put her head back, closed her eyes and basked in the midday sun.

I sat there and thought, *Oh... yes. I remember this.*

~ ~ ~ ~ ~ ~

The last week of my hospitalization at HUP, Adam and I crossed the street to a small park where we had spent time before.

Adam told me to sit down on the ground. I thought nothing of it and proceeded to sit *Indian Style* but, half way down my right leg gave out and I came down with a *thud.* I was embarrassed about it, even though I knew there was nothing to be embarrassed about. The thought of even commenting on what just happened was out of the picture. I was just trying to keep from crying because it hurt. The rest of the time I was trying to find a half way comfortable position. It seemed my body was so tight, especially the right side, every muscle was in a state of trauma and it was *painful.* It was *pain that I felt.* There was *sensation.* I didn't know about the extent of the right-sided weakness. Nobody knew. At these moments my new boundaries were revealed.

More and more, I had been reflecting on the many symptoms I had prior to the bleed, but could not remember to ask any of the doctors around me about the indication of a possible connection. It had gone beyond the memory of the social worker, I had remembered many things, many places I had gone to get answers to what was ailing me. But, I couldn't write a note to myself about it because of my inability to write, or even *think.* Finally, I spoke with Chris about it. We arranged a meeting with Dr. Miaitica, a *physiatrist* at HUP. Chris spoke for me:

"What significance would right-sided tingling and numbing have, the years prior to Madeleine's bleed?"

The doctor indicated tingling and numbing may have been quite significant in determining the outcome. He asked if I had seen any doctors prior to the bleed, I indicated I had, but I could not remember when I had seen them. I felt frustrated at the tardiness of my thought processes, it seemed that I was so close to *knowing* something. But, there were other priorities, the first of whom was a little person named Elizabeth.

~ ~ ~ ~ ~ ~

"I have something for you," Chris said.
"What is it?" I asked.
"Give me your left hand," he said.

I reached forward with my left hand and watched as Chris placed a beautiful diamond ring on my ring finger. I was *shocked.*

Until now, I had forgotten about the ring Chris had given me.

"Do you remember this?" Chris wondered.

I looked at Chris, shaking my head in disbelief. There was so much more about my life that I simply didn't know. I closed my eyes, looked up and said, "Yes............. I..... remember."

~ ~ ~ ~ ~ ~

The week of April 15, 1993, I was on a crash course in getting out of HUP and back into life. I remember quite clearly I was unbelievably scared, but it was time according to the hospital... and the insurance company. Chris had many reservations about my leaving the hospital at this point.

I met with Christine one final time that week and she took back my *shoe buttons* which enabled me to wear sneakers without having to deal with the intricacy of lacing. Two months earlier it wasn't just my inability to manipulate the laces due to my right hand dysfunction but my inability to remember how to make a *bow*. Now, I was able to do it... sort of.

It took me a while to completely understand what AVM bleed *meant*. It also took me a while to absorb the fact that I was *pregnant*, and then delivered a baby and became a *mother*. Just when I thought I was home free, I had to make another choice. I met with Diane a final time on Monday April 19, 1993.

"You have to make a decision about the AVM. There are choices you must make about the AVM," she said.

I was puzzled. "What...... do....... you..... mean? The...... AVM is....... *still*............ in........ there?"

She nodded.

"I...... thought.............. it.... was............... gone!!!"

"The first surgery was to stop the bleed. The AVM is still in there," she said.

It was simply too much. *After all this*... to find out it was still in my brain. I wondered if Chris knew. It was as if I was in a nightmare. I had a decision to make. Diane wrote in my notebook:

1. *surgery*
2. *embolization*
3. *gamma knife - x-ray therapy*

She explained what each of the options involved.

1. *Surgery* to remove the tangle of veins surgically. If the surgery went well, the problem would be gone forever.
2. *Embolization*, or obstructing the flow of blood with a surgical "glue", leaving the AVM inside.
3. *Gamma Knife*, or elimination of the AVM by radiation therapy over time.

I had time to talk about the options with Chris. Time to think. It would be my decision. I felt as if the weight of the world was in my hands.

I said *"good-bye"* to Adam, and others on the 6th floor ...nothing extraordinary as farewell's go, surprisingly. Diane and Christine were out that day, but I was sort of relieved. At that moment I realized something very basic. Some things are just too painful to face.
Don't you know how you have affected my life?
Don't you know how important you are?
*Don't you know that I'll never, **ever** forget you?*
***All** of you!?*
I guess, perhaps... they already knew.

On April 20, 1993, the moment of my departure, all kinds of emotions filled my mind. So happy to be free at last, yet terrified of life ahead. These wonderful people who helped me through such an earth-shattering experience... and there we were, the three of us walking out the doors. They wheeled me out of the emergency room in a wheelchair, as was hospital policy... and that was that. One moment I was a patient, the next... not. Closing one door and opening another.

Chris, Elizabeth and I drove out of HUP and into the university campus towards the Drexel campus. We passed the building in which my interior design course was held almost ten years earlier. A series of flashbacks occurred as I remembered faces and moments in time during my days at Drexel University in 1984. Flashes of the perspective exam, difficulties with the "systems" course and remembering "Sylvia" the head of the design department.

As we passed 30th Street Station, I remembered many commutes to Rhode Island School of Design from 1978 to 1982. Just beyond the train station, was the Philadelphia Art Museum which I had visited in 1986 for the *Monet Exhibit.* Beyond the museum was the Schuyllkil River where I could see the exact location where I had painted scenes of the museum from *East River Drive.* Even further down was Vesper, the **PENN** rowing house where my brother Tony had rowed in high school. We passed the *"Whalen wall,"* the whale mural which had just been completed. Everything looked different, completely different... or maybe I was seeing through different eyes now.

6

The Diagnosis

The first half-hour in my parents' apartment was one flashback after another... *one grande deja-vous.* Everything reflected times out of the past. *Everything* talked to me saying, *"Oh yes... I remember this..."*

First, it was the apartment itself: the layout... the rooms... the views out the windows... furniture... it was all so familiar. It was all that I had grown up with... like an old friend. It was Mom and Dad.

Then, I noticed a small object on a table. It was surrounded by black velvet and it was gold. For some reason I was drawn to it, there was something vaguely familiar about it. I asked my Mother what it was.

"Why... you gave that to me at Christmas... a weeping Buddha," she said.

With that, a deluge of memory flowed into my mind and *goosebumps* covered my body. *A synapse.*

"A weeping Buddha", the woman said in the boutique in Portland, Maine. *I knew it would be a perfect Christmas gift for Mom, and I knew she would appreciate the significance.*

That night, my mother prepared dinner. It required using a knife and fork, which I couldn't do. The meal itself was complex and exhausting, and I found myself becoming extremely irritable. At HUP the food was basic, not complicated... not complex. It hurt to chew this hard, crunchy grainy bread... I couldn't cut this gamey-flavored meat and the dressing on the salad was bitter. Even my taste-buds were affected by the bleed.

Unlike living in the hospital, I began to see how my life had *changed* because of the bleed. I had learned at HUP, my pace was considerably slower because of delays in thought processes and nearly non-functional use of my right hand. Everything I did was backwards. Even when I tried to compensate, it was to no avail. I knew that I was different, I just kept trying to find myself again. I could see it in the communication with my parents, but there was nothing I could do.

A few days went by... During a conversation with Dad, Mom and Chris, I referred to my condition as a stroke. Dad informed me that I did *not* have a stroke rather, a congenital malfunction similar to an aneurysm. I was confused once again. Dad said I had an Arteriovenous Malformation, which caused a stroke.

I sat there for a moment, allowing my memory to find the route.

"A.V.M," I said.

Everyone looked at me. Didn't they understand what I was trying to say? That was Leslie's diagnosis in 1989, at the Hospital in Portsmouth, New Hampshire. The tremendously overwhelming diagnosis. Finally, I discovered my problem. What they had always known, I had only just learned. Oh, the tangled webs we weave. It had taken what seemed like a lifetime to understand.

"AVM............ was........... Leslie's................... original......... diag...nosis."

~ ~ ~ ~ ~ ~

Mom thought it would be a good idea to involve me in the dinner preparation, and asked me to make the salad one night. *The problem was*, I was unable to focus with Mom talking, but I did. *The problem was*, I was unable use my right hand to cut vegetables, but I tried. *The problem was*, there was so much visual stimulation in the kitchen that I couldn't remain focussed on anything for more than a few seconds, but I didn't want to give-up in front of my mother. Finally, after two hours, the task was completed. So was I, and it made me angry. I could no longer function and just stopped performing. I kept forgetting about my limited stamina.

A week after leaving HUP, while putting on my jeans my right leg gave out. After not having any feeling for so long, suddenly... I had feeling. The sensation was *unbelievable*. As I fell, I tried to break the impact with my right hand. I screamed because of the pain, Chris came to me but I couldn't tell him where the pain was orginating *from*. There were intense shooting pains from my feet to my fingers on my right side but it was *delayed pain*. I would suffer every third second. Chris noticed I was favoring my right hand, he put the baby in the carriage and we drove to the hospital. (The ambulance driver would not take us to HUP.) I tried to keep the screaming within, as I didn't want to scare Elizabeth, but the pain was unbearable. When we got to the emergency room at HUP, my right hand was the focal area.

The ER doctor asked what had happened, but, I couldn't get my words out. I knew exactly what happened but the phraseology was blocked. Just like *The Berlin Wall:* an entire country separated by an impenetrable concrete wall: my spoken words were separated by an impenetrable, *invisible* wall in my own mind.

An X-ray revealed a break in my right wrist, and a cast was made covering the entire arm. I was more worried about Chris at the time. After going through *all he had been faced with,* from then on I knew every single thing I did had to be *well thought out.* Once again, I didn't realize the severity of the right-sided weakness until then. It was my new reality.

Unlike living in the hospital, now I began to comprehend what my new life would be. I was learning my daily pace was considerably slower because of delays in thought processes and nearly nonfunctional use of my right hand. In addition, everything I did was backwards. I also found that I couldn't solve mathematical problems... even very basic ones. All my bookkeeping from my gallery came to mind but I couldn't place that in time in relation to my life.

Could that have been ten years ago?

I asked Chris when I owned the gallery and was stunned to find out it was only six months ago that I closed it.

I knew I was different. I just kept trying to find myself again. I could see it in the communication with my parents, there didn't seem to be anything I could do about it. As in any reasonably healthy family, there were tensions during such a tumultuous time. For my parents, it was like a cruel time warp. It had only been three years since the birth of my sister's child, followed by my sister's death three weeks later.

One of the first things I noticed in the relationship with my parents was everything to them had so much more meaning than before. They thought I had become more intelligent. It was my abilities to communicate (...or lack of) that they were responding to, in that every time I spoke all ears were focused on me. Everything I said was brief and concise. It was a struggle making any points in conversation because I couldn't respond quickly enough to be part of a discussion.

Chris, Elizabeth and I went out driving and walking every day. Chris was the pilot, Elizabeth was the comic relief and I was the navigator. For me, driving a car was out of the picture: it would be very dangerous. It wasn't just the visual blockage which hadn't improved, it was my delayed responses and lack of confidence. I tried remembering my way around, but more than half the time I was *winging-it*, as my sense of direction had been affected by the bleed.

Nearly everyday, I walked up 24th Street to a city park, accompanied by either my Dad or Chris. Being outside was of great importance to me. It allowed me to continue with physical therapy, but also forced me to continue re-developing my confidence, manner and sense-of-being. Dad was patient and kind and always considerate. My mind and body would fatigue in a matter of minutes frequently on the walks and there was nothing that could change it.

We ventured out to all my old haunts, Valley Forge Park, Bryn Mawr, Narberth, Gladwyne, the Court at King of Prussia and the whole *Main Line*. I took them to see all the places I had lived in my life, the houses I grew-up in and the apartments I lived in after graduating from RISD. They saw my nursery school, elementary, jr. high and high school. I showed them streams that you drive through

116

and the parks that I played in. It was all the same and I was grateful for that. I kept thinking how thankful I was to be where I had grown-up.

We drove to my grandparents house which had been sold after my grandfather died. *When was that*? I thought. *Gramma died two years before Grampa. It was after Doug died... Doug died in 1986... Gramma died shortly after that... and then Grampa. Grampa died a month before I moved to Maine.* I kept trying to place myself in time. It didn't matter though, it was still Gramma and Grampa's house. It was not a figment of my imagination; it was real. It was the first time I had been able to show Chris where I had grown-up. He began to understand a deeper level of my background and how I came to be the person he knew.

~ ~ ~ ~ ~ ~

Soon, Chris and I made an appointment with Dr. Kotapka to discuss my decision and how I should proceed. I was lucky to *have* a choice. We met in Dr. Kotapka's office at the hospital and I told him that I chose surgery. It was time. I seemed to have complete faith in Dr. Kotapka, after all, he saved my life... and Elizabeth's too. He had become somewhat of an idol in my mind. I felt the need to let him complete what he had begun. From the moment I began realizing what he was to me, I couldn't stop thinking about him. I felt this obsession was normal, and I tried to keep it to myself. I was well aware of the risk at that point. I didn't want the AVM in my brain... *in my life*, any longer.

On June 2, 1993, Chris, Elizabeth and I checked into HUP once again. There were many faces from an earlier time of year wanting to wish me well, including Adam, Diane and Christine from *Ravdin*. I hadn't seen anyone since leaving the sixth floor rehab and seeing them now, felt bittersweet. My feelings towards them were very powerful: love foremost, but also frustration, dependence, pride, anger, pain... It was all there, once again.

Chris and Elizabeth stayed for awhile but at 9 P.M., we said good-bye.

The next morning was the big day. Chris showed-up at 7 A.M.. I was so happy to see him... it was a surprise to me. I forgot

Chris told me he would see me in the morning. Everything was a surprise to me since the bleed. Life was so different and although my mind had settled down since December 27, 1992, none-the-less my mind was altered. I only hoped I would continue to see improvements.

The Phenobarbital shielded me from anxiety over the fact that I was minutes away from an operation that may permanently change my thought processes forever. They had already been changed by the initial bleed but this time, I was *conscious*.

By the time I was wheeled out of my room, the "block" had completely numbed my body from the waist down. I didn't fully understand how it was all going to be done, but I wasn't about to start asking now.

Chris was by my side. We said good-bye to each other, held each other's' stare for a spell.

"See you in a while..."

Then, we both said *"I love you..."* The thought, the memory of that moment is rooted in my soul.

~ ~ ~ ~ ~ ~

7

Long Way

I woke to the sound of someone vomiting. I was thinking how terrible it sounded. The person was unable to stop vomiting. Suddenly, I realized the person who was vomiting was me. The bitter taste was on my tongue and down my throat. A nurse was tending to me and I felt helpless in my inability to clean-up. Then... I remembered where I was.

"I made it... Thank you, God... thank you."
I went under again.

A while later, there was a man's voice. I opened my eyes and there was Dr.Kotapka. He smiled and said, "The AVM is gone."

My entire body tingled at his words. I closed my eyes tightly, looked up and whispered, "Thank you..." There was so much more to say.

Dr Kotapka said, "Sleep..."
So, I did.

~ ~ ~ ~ ~ ~

Everyone was on *cloud 9*. I needed time to myself though... with Chris and Elizabeth.

Elizabeth seemed to know something had happened to "Mommy". She was confused by my absences, and her little forehead *had a furl.* After that, I became very loving and protective towards her, more than ever before. My priorities changed after seeing Elizabeth's little concerned face. For the first time since she was born, I could see my role as *Mommy*, and I didn't want my child to worry about *me.* In the middle of the scene the spotlight fell on Elizabeth. Suddenly, a new perspective came into view: my baby needed *me* and I needed *her.*

As happy as everyone was, I needed peace and quiet. My perceptions had become more intense because of the surgery. Noises were more intense, voices penetrated and everything seemed to echo even more than before. I was overwhelmed by the intensity of everything. I wanted to share the happy outcome with everyone, but at one point, it was all too intense. Seven people were in my room, someone startled me with a kiss on my cheek and *the floodwaters broke through.* It was too much stimulation, I needed silence. Silence was all I could handle.

It was the 9th floor: *Neuro Recovery.* It was where I had spent time in the early days out of the coma but I didn't remember anything about the floor. After three days, I was moved from the observation room to a standard room, also on the neuro recovery floor. Each morning, I was taken via wheelchair to the 1st floor, also a rehab floor. I washed and dressed although I seemed to be the only one to bother. The other patients were content to wear their robes but I had the *one-foot-out-the-door* approach. I could almost taste the freedom.

I spent my days walking on the ninth floor or basking in the air-conditioned splendor of the family waiting room. It was Philadelphia in June and it was stifling. I listened to my tapes, although half of them were foreign to my ears until I played them thirty times. Just like everything else, slowly with time and repetition the music that was once familiar to me, slowly became familiar again. A musician friend of mine sent his new tape through the mail. Tears filled my eyes as I played the tape. It was my friend's voice, my friend's music. I remembered his performances: Kennebunkport, York, South Berwick... his music, was home.

And in the never ending rhythm
Of the waves along the bay
There are things I notice now
And you can hear
These promises of life
Spirit lived

Stephen Bracciotti

During the period of nursing, the body must be able to provide nutrients for both the baby and the mother. In the morning, I used the breast pump and stored Elizabeth's "lunch" in the refrigerator. One morning, after breakfast of pancakes and sausage, my system rejected the food. I felt shaky and weak, and just then the hospital escort had come to my room to wheel me down to my scheduled rehab on the first floor. Within minutes after arriving, I became powerless. No one knew about my system rejecting breakfast. Suddenly, I couldn't stand, and I was unable to explain this sudden weakness to the therapist. I didn't quite know what was happening myself, only that I didn't want to tell everyone in the room about the effect breakfast had on my digestive tract. This was not the sixth floor, I didn't know these therapists, and I couldn't communicate. The therapist must have thought I just needed a little help, as she kept telling me to *stand*. Finally, I collapsed like a ragdoll. I managed to communicate that I wasn't feeling well, and eventually I was wheeled back to my room. It was alarming to me that even *now*, I was not able to take care of myself simply because I was unable to speak fluently. *How am I going to make it out there?*

The anxiety and depression were overwhelming when I was alone. Even when there were people about, I felt it knawing at my psyche. It had diminished considerably since the awakening, but moments alone were still difficult. There was always the voice in my mind, *Hold on, hold on, hold on*, just as there was at the beginning. I did notice improvements and I was looking forward to getting back to Maine, although I didn't remember too much about it.

We would have to continue living with my parents. We couldn't leave yet. We needed their help and their support. We tried not to step on each other's delicate little toes. It would be another six weeks.

The last day of my hospital stay, I was heading back to my room, walking very cautiously. The strength and feeling in my right foot had regressed slightly and my balance was affected since the final surgery. As I walked down the corridor there was Dr. Langer, one of the residents whom I had seen every week while I was at HUP. He was watching me walk and function, and I was trying so hard not to fall or stumble. As I passed him, he smiled. No words were spoken, but it seemed something was said.

Nine days after the final surgery to remove the AVM, I left HUP. I would need to return again in six weeks, to see if further surgery would be required. Until then, I would be an outpatient at MAGEE Rehab, in Philadelphia.

~ ~ ~ ~ ~ ~

MADELEINE

CHRIS

I CANT WAIT TO GET BACK

MAINE

MAINE

MARIE

MAD

We went to Magee Rehab three times a week for PT, OT and speech therapy. During the very first meeting with one of the placement directors at Magee, I was once again overwhelmed at my inability to communicate. Chris thought I would be able to give an overview of my condition, but no words would come. Once again I knew what needed to be said, but my brain would not cooperate. I hated these moments, when I would literally have to *prove* my illness to those unfamiliar with my condition. Inevitably, I wound-up sobbing in front of a perfect stranger and felt *diminished* because of it. How could they know what my life had been before the bleed? How could they possibly feel empathy? They couldn't, and once again, *like a magician*, I would try to pull myself together *"right before their very eyes."*

At Magee, Carol, the PT had me walking... *walking very quickly.* I had relearned basic movements during my inpatient days at HUP but at Magee, the physical therapy was almost a *contradiction* from that which I had learned from Adam and I was confused about that. I realized I was not in a position to question the structure of the program, at Magee... *or anywhere.* These people were *doing good things.* Instead of resisting, I began to allow them to help me. I had strong emotional bonds leftover from my HUP days, so I tried to focus on the present.

I was surprised to know what I was capable of in physical therapy. It was more of a whole body therapy, focusing on spontaneous movement, stretching and strengthening.

Suddenly, I realized I had done these exercises with a doctor in Portland, Maine. He couldn't figure-out what was wrong, but week after week I worked with him. I remembered feeling embarrassed that nothing seemed to be the cause... When did I see this doctor? Was he even a doctor?

I had trouble keeping my schedule straight with the speech therapist at Magee. There was always a change of location of her office, perhaps that in itself was part of the therapy. Either way, because of that I missed much speech therapy time. Chris *also* was confused about the constant changes in the time allotted for speech therapy.

My OT, Shriling, was from China on an exchange program. One day, I was to prepare lunch. I gave her the list of food items she was to purchase. It was to be thinly sliced breast of chicken, dipped in batter and lightly fried, served with rice. The day of the lunch, she arrived with chicken legs and thighs, announcing the chicken breasts were too expensive. *How was she to know how I felt about the blood vessels in dark meat? How was she to know that the gamey flavor of dark meat was not appealing to me?* I indicated the dark meat would do and I tried to *sweep it under the rug...* only, it seemed that I couldn't. By the time the meat was finished cooking, I had worked myself into a "tizzy". My temper had flared and before anyone could blink, I threw out the fully prepared chicken, cleaned the pots and dishes and swept the floor. It was a moment I would just as soon forget... if only I could.

One day at Magee a new patient arrived; she had been in a car accident. The woman was sitting at a table across from me and she was just staring at her own hand and arm. She was clearly in a state of shock. I watched her for a while, her expression revealed the horror of a debilitating accident... and I had great empathy for her.

Our friends Lori and Jim, had us over for lunch one afternoon in July. They had visited me at HUP a few times and even had Chris spend the night once when I was in the coma. Their house was located on a steep incline accessible via steps... *with no railing.* It was an "Adam Walk," one which Chris and I had so named for the conditions or obstacles that Adam, my PT at HUP would subject me to in an effort to increase my awareness of potential problems I may encounter while walking. Chris helped me up the steps at Lori and Jim's, but I just wanted them to disappear while I struggled.

The lunch itself was fine, yet difficult. Everything was always so difficult. Inability to taste the food, noises, vision... were different now. No one seemed to be aware of the difficulties I was encountering that afternoon. I felt isolated... but aware.

Chris and I worked like a team. If I had something to say, I would begin talking and inevitably be interrupted, at which time I would lose my *train of thought.* Then, I looked at Chris to indicate I had forgotten the conversation... or simply ask what I was just talking about. It was constant, in that it would happen every five seconds. I didn't want to let on that I couldn't keep track of running conversations because I felt that I would continue to improve... or find new ways to compensate. It was exhausting. We left their house or *wherever* we may be, and I would cry immediately because it took so much to *perform*. I told Chris after we left, I couldn't *taste* the lunch we had just eaten. It was hard to look ahead to the future because the present was so hard to take. The past became a source of inspiration for my destiny.

Shortly after the lunch with Lori and Jim, we ran into another old friend of mine at a mall. My friend, Janet and I were next-door neighbors from birth. She and her husband lived in Connecticut, and were visiting family for the weekend. She didn't recognize me at first, as she was focused on Elizabeth in the carriage. When she realized it was me, the look on her face revealed her shock. She did not disregard me... and that meant *so much*. It was as if she fully understood the *hell* I was going through. It was more than her seeing me walking with a cane, I could see she clearly conceived the change, both physically and cognitively. I felt self-conscious and embarrassed. I didn't want her... or anyone to see me like this.

I had great difficulty communicating, which was evident. Chris did the talking for me. My old friend knew of the coma and Elizabeth's birth, she had just given birth to her first child as well. She and I had spoken over the telephone just a week prior to my illness, which I had forgotten. I wondered if she knew of my inability to write? Perhaps, she knew.

~ ~ ~ ~ ~ ~

At the end of July, once again Chris and I went back to HUP for the follow-up scan. A type of dye was injected into my system via the main artery located in the crotch of the body. The dye travels through the system and eventually reaches the brain. I felt a strange warmth throughout my body, specifically in my head and groin and a *queasy* sensation in my stomach. A projection screen is used to allow the surgeon to view my brain... and where the AVM had been. The bizarre thing is, *I watched the procedure* while I lay there. Towards the end, the tension became overwhelm-

129

ing and I began to weep. The nurses became alarmed and I quickly realized the severity of the slightest movement *by me*, might cause the most damage of all.

After another twenty minutes, the procedure was completed. The doctors and nurses broke down the equipment, while I lay still on the exam table, realizing the images were in the process of review.

Suddenly, one of the surgeons opened the door.

"We have to go back in," he stated, with urgency. He closed the door again.

It felt as if someone had punched me in the stomach. I felt empty... and incredibly sad. I knew it meant they had found something of significance. *How could it be* that I lead a healthy life and have it suddenly taken away? I thought about Chris and Elizabeth and how I wanted all the turmoil to end. All the hell that we'd been through since December 27, 1992. I have lived a *life* in this body. It has been through so much. Why is this happening? It's a good mind! It's a healthy body! *Please let it end... What's in there?* I thought it was *me?!*

I felt distanced from my body, but I wanted to give it support, like a fallen athlete. I just had to lay there, in silence. The room was very cold.

Finally, after about twenty minutes, one of the surgeons came in again.

"It's okay, we won't need to do another surgery."

I still felt I couldn't relax until I was out of the operating room. At last, it was time to go home.

The next day, the three of us left for Maine. It was July 26, 1993. It had been seven months since I left for the Christmas visit.

~ ~ ~ ~ ~ ~

8

The Precious Jewel

The following morning we left Philadelphia and headed North, following my parents to Bopci's house in Massachusetts. At the age of 91, my grandmother still cooked dinner for the four of us. Everything was just as I remembered in Bopci's house. Figurines on the mantle were dusted and in place... the spiral stair banister... the red and white enamel kitchen table... but it was all *surreal*. Just like a dream. Still, it was so familiar. Just as revisiting the towns of my childhood, everything was born again.

The next day, we crossed the Piscataqua River bridge in Portsmouth, New Hampshire which marks the border into Maine. *Maine, the way life should be.*

Again, a series of flashbacks came to mind as we headed home. We took the main highway *95 North*, and then Route One through York, Cape Neddick, Ogunquit and Wells, all of which were home to me. *It seemed like a dream... I had been living a life here.*

Chris kept asking, "Do you remember this?"

I kept saying, "Yes..." I didn't know *how* I remembered things, I just did.

I was more than satisfied with the rental house, especially because the master bedroom was on the first floor. It was a cape in a nice little neighborhood with sidewalks. No *Adam walks*... for a while. The next day we drove to our apartment located in a large

133

farmhouse and Chris pulled into the driveway. We were home. Chris and I had a moment of clarity, as we gathered our wits, dried our tears and ventured up to the apartment with Elizabeth.

Everything was just the same and I knew that. The life that I had was clarified once again. All the touches in the apartment said, *"Where've you been? We've missed you..."* After a moment of realization, Chris and I pulled ourselves together.

I just painted the walls last year...
This bookcase is new...
I framed this painting a month before Christmas...

In my studio, there was a project which I just completed prior to my Christmas trip: a redesign of a storefront for a building in York, Maine. There were completed architectural drawings for another job I had done earlier in 1992. There were watercolor paintings I did in the fall of 1992, as well as other watercolors and oil paintings I just framed prior to the December trip. Pen and ink menus I had done. There were boxes of hand-painted Christmas ornaments that I sold at craft fairs in November and December 1992. There were two crates of supplies for my gallery, *title/medium/cost* cards for paintings, the daily log, the guest book, etc. It was everything that was my life as I looked around my studio. Photos of Chris... photos of "Mr. Spike" my cat... all of my framing supplies, glass, mat cutters, blades, paint, brushes and frames. *My studio.* I just stood there taking it all in and remembering everything as I scanned the room.

I did the same visual processing in each room of the apartment. It was stimulating... overwhelming and emotionally trying as all of my accomplishments, *all of my life* was revealed. I thought about Diane, Adam and Christine, my therapists' at HUP.

This is what I do!!! This is who I am!!!
But, all I could do was take it all in, in silence.

After an hour or so, as I continued to reacquaint myself with everything, I opened a chest and found files... *medical insurance files.* Page by page, I sorted through the papers, all in chronological order beginning in 1990. I saw doctors, physical therapists and chiropractors. I began remembering specific phone conversations with the insurance claim adjusters, concerned about my chronic disorder... and the expense of my problem. Finally, it was determined my condition was psychological. As I reviewed each page... it all became clear. The tingling... the numbing... was the harbinger of things to come.

I began to have multitudes of memory synapses, all related to the insurance paperwork in my hands. Even other episodes seemingly unrelated came to mind.

The headaches...
The right sided numbing and tingling...
The twisting...
The weakness...

Every specialist I had seen was unable to pinpoint the problem. I had worked with eight medical professionals, often, for a few months at a time. Like an avalanche in my mind, memories of countless interactions with doctors and therapists flooded my mind.

The honeymoon numbing *and illness...*
The shooting pain up the back of my head, then clear down to my right foot... then the deadening feeling...

I thought about the conversation with Dr. Miatica my last week at HUP, in which he indicated the tingling fingers and arm may be related to the bleed. My memory was impaired to the extent that there was no short-term memory while I was at HUP, and even long-term memory had been altered. But, it wasn't my foot, or hand or back... *it was my brain.* Now, it appeared to me there was meaning to it all. I could see that I had *tried* to find the meaning. That knowledge alone... was like a precious jewel. It told me that no matter what, I wouldn't stop searching for the answer and in that... I found myself, again.

Chris moved everything out of our apartment that week and we said good-bye to the place we had called "home" for four years. It would be too dangerous to navigate the stairs on a daily basis especially with the "little one." We would rent a house for the time being, until one would be built for us. Oddly, we had most of our belongings in boxes already. Days before the Christmas visit seven months earlier, we decided against a house rental but we had all our possessions ready to go. It was a strange feeling, like a premonition of the fated journey.

At the beginning of August 1993, we rented a cottage for five days on Lake Winnepesaukee in New Hampshire. Just to be away from *all* that was so restricting, made me realize how oppressive my life had become. Still, I understood that I *did* have limitations and that I would have to prove myself worthy of independence, and it made me angry. But, there was a constant fear in my gut that I would fail. That I would never make it back to what I knew... to my life. Then I would focus on Elizabeth and Chris, and that forced me to forget about *me*.

My days at the lake with Chris and Elizabeth were fun and relaxing. Finally, Chris and I found the beginnings of happiness again.

Back home, Chris arranged my continuing rehab at "Bayside" in Portland forty-five minutes away. Therapy involved speech, occupational and physical therapy just as before. Once again, it was difficult making the transition and I felt like an outsider. I wanted to be accepted for who I had been, but I was definitely still on the outside looking in.

I began feeling *trapped.* Now it was my home, my territory... but I felt as if I couldn't breathe. All of the freedoms I once had in Maine were gone because of my condition. *Everything I did*, I did accompanied by a guardian. If Chris was to be working, arrangements were made for my supervision. I wanted to break-free of the restrictions, just as an animal entrapped. It was a problem, as everyone was concerned about Elizabeth's well-being.

After three months of supervision and no mistakes on my part, I discussed the lack of freedom issue with Chris. It was decided I would take care of our child without further supervision.

I asked Chris to set-up an appointment with an opthamologist for me. The visual blockage, of which I had sought medical attention at HUP, had not improved. The diagnosis was as I had anticipated: my field of vision was damaged by the bleed. The vision area of the human brain was located in the area of my hemorrhage. The test revealed I had lost 25% of my sight, permanently... but not focal vision, only the peripheral. The implications were staggering, and I was so thankful that the damage was not more extensive.

~ ~ ~ ~ ~ ~

In October, we went to the mountains. They were so beautiful, as they always have been, but everything seemed to have new meaning now. Everything was also frightening now. My mind and body had come so close to *ceasing*, I seemed to be in a state of *red alert*. My self-confidence was gone, too. It was as if I was living in a nightmare, one that is so real I kept wanting to wake-up to break-out of the confines of the dream, in order to see that it was only a dream. For the time, here in the mountains, far from rehab.. far from restrictions and far from the reality of my struggles... I found peace.

Christmas was a confusing blur. My inability to focus made life impossible. It became a matter of trying to stay in *a straight line*. Just keep doing the same things everyday. Build a daily pattern to keep from becoming disoriented.

The new year was most welcome. It had been a year since the bleed.

~ ~ ~ ~ ~ ~

In January 1994, I decided to switch my physical therapy to York Hospital. It was fifteen minutes away, as opposed to the forty-five minute trek to Portland while I continued the cognitive therapy at Bayside once a week. Chris drove me three days a week, for an hour of therapy. When we returned home, I napped until Chris woke me, unless I set the music alarm. Often times, I napped twice in a day, especially if it was the weekly food shopping day in Portsmouth. One day, as we passed a small mall on the way to the hospital, I had a flashback of an appointment with an optometrist in the mall.

"I'm nervous doctor," I said.
"Why are you nervous?"
"My sister, Leslie, had gone for a new prescription for

eyeglasses in 1989, because she was "seeing double". She was also six and a half months pregnant. Her optometrist told her to call her doctor immediately once he saw her optic nerve. That's when he knew it was brain related. I'm afraid what you might find," I said.

"What was it that your sister had?" the optometrist asked.

"Well, after about a month of CT scans, her doctors diagnosed it as an A.V.M. But, it turned out to be basal cell melanoma, and she died three weeks after the baby was born."

"I'm sorry. I'll tell you if I see anything."

"It's just that... I'm six months pregnant now, just where Leslie was three years ago. I'm a little nervous."

He began the examination, first the left eye, then the right. He hesitated.

"Hmmph..."

"What is it?" I asked.

He didn't answer. What is it that he can see? I waited for a response, then he said, "Probably nothing."

"Are you sure? You frightened me!"

"Everything looks fine," he said.

Perhaps, I should go in and tell him that it *was* something significant, but what would I say? ***What would I say?!***

Again, I began having flashbacks of visits to an occupational therapist whom I had seen prior to the bleed regarding my tingling and numbing hand. One day, I ran into her. I tried to communicate my situation. I felt uncomfortable about my inability to judge whether talking about what had happened to me would in some way would imply fault. So, I tried to keep it to myself from then on.

One afternoon in February, Chris's mother picked me up after therapy at the hospital. On the way home, I asked her if we could drive by a building I had designed in 1992. It was difficult communicating to her the fact that I had created the structure. We drove there and sure enough, it was completed. All the details were done to specification, even the suggested landscaping was finished according to the plan I had done the preceding year.

The following week, I asked Chris to drive by all of the projects I had completed since 1990. We started with the Massachusetts anesthesiologist whose house was done in Spring 1992, then another re-design also from 1992. We stopped for lunch at the restaurant I had re-designed in 1990, and we ran into the contractor I had worked with on most of those jobs! It was an awkward moment as my speech deficit hindered the flow of the conversation. Finally, we left the restaurant and drove by the site of the last job I did prior to the bleed: an A&P grocery store conversion. I redesigned the store to a *mini-mall*, which also was completed. The afternoon was stimulating and draining but left me with an incentive: I wanted my life back.

One day, as I went through some boxes searching for drafting supplies, I happened upon an award I had received in 1990. It was for a design I had done while working at Kenneth Parker Associates in Philadelphia in 1987. I had never framed this award, probably because I didn't see the *point* at the time. I had *forgotten* about the award, but now, there was definitely a point. It was the *Interior Business Design Award* for the Price Waterhouse job, in Falls Church, Virginia. The IBD award is one of the highest honors in the business. Suddenly, there was a point.

Everyday I walked through the neighborhood. One time, because of my visual impairment, I didn't see a German shepherd dog coming at me until it was within biting distance. I screamed and fell to the ground in trauma. I couldn't get a handle on myself and I just lay there on the street sobbing for a few minutes. I limped back to the house in shock and Chris walked over to confront the owner. The man wasn't the least bit affected by Chris's concern.

After three months of PT at York Hospital, I was given photo-copies of the forty exercises I was to continue on a daily basis. I always did exercises prior to the bleed but now I couldn't remember what exercises I did or how to do them. My mind drew a blank and I was embarrassed to ask Chris, as I knew it was a simple exercise. Not only did I forget how to do them but I couldn't remember what area of my body the exercise focused on. I only knew that I used to do exercises. One day, I finally asked Chris if he remembered seeing me do the exercises.

"What was that exercise I used to do all the time?"

"Were you standing or sitting?" Chris asked.

"I think I was lying down" I said.

"Like this?" Chris demonstrated.

"Yes! That's the one that I've always done! What's that called, again?" I asked.

"It's a sit-up" Chris said.

"*Oh brother!* That's a *sit-up*? All this time I've been trying to remember a stupid sit-up?" I shook my head in disgust. I sat there thinking, *How am I ever going to be able to get-it-all-back, when I can't even remember the simplicity of a sit-up?*

~ ~ ~ ~ ~ ~

I began a daily journal at Christmas, but with therapy, Elizabeth, exercises, walking, cleaning and cooking there was *no time to write*. Finally, I managed to block off time for writing.

May 1994
S M T W T F S
1 2 3 4 5 6 7
8 9 10 11 12 13 14
15 16 17 18 19 20 21
22 23 24 25 26 27 28
29 30 31

7 Last night, as I was dozing off
to sleep, I remembered the
8 day I woke up at H.U.P.
I was on the 9th floor.
9 the nurses station was just
outside my room. My mother
10 was with me, to my right.
I remember Chris ~~coming in~~
~~calling on the phone~~

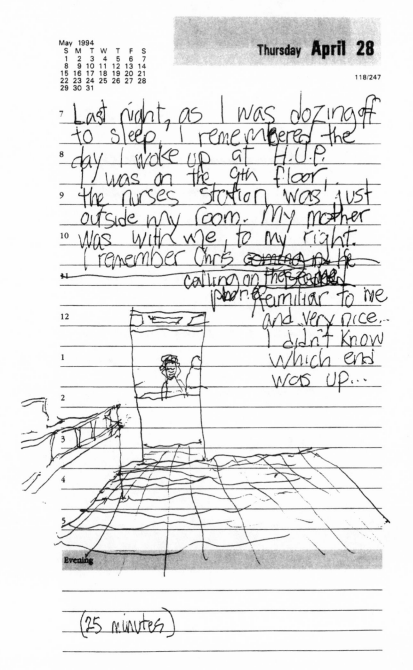

familiar to me
and very nice...
I didn't know
which end
was up...

(25 minutes)

141

April 30, 1994

Everything in life is taken for granted, but when you have a brain injury, you are faced with beginning again... not completely... at least in my case, but in many ways, beginning again. Like being born again. I still don't know how I used to put my shoes on.

(21 minutes)

At the bottom of the page, I usually wrote the amount of time that it took me to write the excerpt. I felt it was necessary in an effort to gauge my progress. In my mind, without gauging myself, there would be no incentive to improve. Even in writing, it is grossly apparent that something was terribly wrong. At least, I had to try. In February 1993, my fingers were too weak to hold a pencil. It just made me fight even more.

When I was at HUP, I noticed a change in the relationships with both of my brothers, but I didn't understand exactly *why* the relationships had changed. It began to clarify as time and continued therapy passed. I began trying to rationalize the effects of the bleed. I could clearly see that the area of my brain that had been most severely damaged was also the same area that dealt with my brother Tony, as well as my mother. I had great difficulty remembering *who they were* during the first year of recovery. It forced me to see my entire family individually, or separately as the bleed had wiped away part of my mind. *It was gone.* Bringing that part of me back meant constant internal searching in order to re-route areas of my mind that had been destroyed.

Both of my brothers and I, spoke over the phone about once a month, post AVM bleed. They were alarmed at my grave medical condition. One even had a brain scan to confirm the absence of any malfunction. It was difficult talking about it with them because I was still healing and my body was in a state of *constant alarm*. None-the-less, I asked questions about my state-of-being each time we conversed. At one point, Tony and I were talking about an instance at HUP directly after the coma began. He told me my eyes popped open during his farewell as he spoke about Doug, my late first husband. Initially, there was no memory of this *awakening*, but later that night just as I dozed off to sleep, I experienced the flashback. The next morning, I called Tony in Seattle.

"I remembered, Tony," I said.

"I don't know, Maddie... maybe you would *like* to remember, but..." his skepticism reflected in his tone.

"You were in my face, Tony. You were within inches of my face... and it startled me... *right?*" I said.

"Yes, that's right," Tony said. "Wow, you *remember* that?"

"I do. As clear as I'm remembering right now. You were so

surprised, and said something like, *"Maddie, you can hear me? We have all been so worried..."* Immediately, I slipped back into the coma. The thing is, I didn't know who you were, Tony. It was like I was just a vessel that could hear... and remember a past."

I sensed Tony's ambivalence... but I didn't mind. I knew my thoughts, and that was all that mattered.

9

Sand Castles

In May 1994, we moved into our first house. I continued therapy in Portland. There were necessary expenses such as window treatments, paint, etc., that we incurred, and I began to relearn budget issues. I began to see more clearly too, in a cognitive sense. Still, in dealing with the general public again, I was also having to contend with the *ignorance* of the general public. Very quickly, I found the need for discretion of the utmost importance. It was difficult, as the bleed and my HUP days were at the forefront of my thoughts.

I still had the startle reaction problem as I had during my HUP days but was able to keep it under control most of the time. It seemed as long as I was aware of potential problems I managed to make it through the days. The first month in the new house was unsettling because of my paranoia. I knew the anxiety was caused by the brain damage, so again I tried to focus on that realization. Fatigue and depression were chronic. One of our neighbors was a bird hunter and would fire blanks to prepare his dogs for hunting season. Each shot he fired took three years off my life. Even with our windows closed, the sound penetrated my ears and startled my brain.

Over the course of time that first year, I was weaned off Phenobarbital. Still, I noticed a definite contrast in my thought processes. Somehow, the memory of who I had been kept revealing itself. Friends and family reassured me of my actions constantly. I found my self-consciousness extremely annoying.

I began working on a letter directed to the doctors' and therapists I had seen prior to the bleed. I needed to communicate the end result of my intensive search for answers. However, making points and reaching conclusions was lacking in my communication ability. It seemed impossible to write the letter but after a month, it became a priority. Writing itself was difficult because of my inability to spell, not to mention the fact that my thoughts were vacating my mind within seconds. Finally, after three months, I completed the letter. After all that it took to write it, there were no responses.

August 26, 1994

Dear Doctor,

I sought your services sometime between 1989 and 1992.

On December 27, 1992, while visiting family in Philadelphia, I had a bleed in my head (Arteriovenus Malformation). It left me comatose for 5 weeks. I was six months pregnant at the time.

When I first woke, I had no idea that I was pregnant or that I was even married. I thought I was a little girl about 8 years old. Everyday was like 3 days to my "inner clock" and every minute I would forget what I had done just a minute before. My right side was completely inert and I couldn't walk, write, talk (sensibly) or eat. I was a different person. It was pretty horrific.

A woman I had never seen before kept showing-up. Every day she would show-up and every day she would sit in the chair by the bed and I would try to remember who she was. And after a couple minutes the word "MOM" would come out of my mouth. I'd say to myself, "Holy Toledo." The next six months I spent recovering in Philadelphia.

I'm working with the folks at Bayside rehab in Portland, ME

now. I've been going once a week for a year now. They've been great. My husband Chris, has been like a rock. He has been with me every day since this happened and has done his best to make sure I've been receiving the best possible care.

Our baby is wonderful! Elizabeth Anna is her name. She is healthy and full of life.

It's been a long road back, a road that I am still on, and probably will be for a long time. But... Elizabeth and I are alive, and that's okay by me. Every week I see improvement and I'm hoping to get back to architectural design work again.

In closing, I believe there is a correlation between all the symptoms that I was having in 1989, 1990, 1991 and 1992 and the AVM bleed.

"AVM's are hemorrhages from abnormal tangles of blood vessels, often causing severe headaches, hemi-paresis and other dysfunctioning of one side of the brain and possibly epilepsy. Symptoms may occur over a long period of time, often years, if not diagnosed." *

I'm hoping this insight will possibly help others who have symptoms similar to mine that are difficult to diagnose.

Please feel free to call or write if you have any questions.

Sincerely,

Madeleine P. Hopkins
(phone #)

CC:
(1990) Dr. X, York, ME (re: right hand)
(1990) Therapist X, @ X Hospital (re: right hand)
(1990) Dr. X, Portsmouth, NH (re: right hand and arm)
(1990) Dr. X, Massachusetts General Hospital, Boston
            (re: right hand arm and shoulder)
(1990) Dr. X, Portland, ME (re: right hand, arm,
            shoulder and right side of back)
(1991) Dr. X, Kennebunk, ME (re: right hand, arm,
            shoulder and right side of back)
(1991) Dr. X, Portland, ME (re: right hand, arm,
            shoulder, leg, right side of back and neck)
(1991) Dr. X, Portland, ME (re: right hand, arm
            shoulder, leg, right side of back and neck)
(1992) Dr. X, Moody, ME (complete physical)

(1992) L.C.S.W., Wells, ME
(1992) Dr. Kotapka, Philadelphia, PA
       (re: Arteriovenus Malformation bleed, ER
       surgery)
(1992) Magee Rehab, Philadelphia, PA
       (rehab from AVM bleed)
(1993 to present)
       Bayside Rehab, Portland, ME
       (rehab from AVM bleed)

Through This Window: Views on Traumatic Brain Injury.
Edited by Patricia I. Felton,
Published by EBTS, Inc.,
North Waterboro, ME.

Chris, Elizabeth and I headed down to Philadelphia in September 1994 for a family wedding. I arranged several other meetings with friends as well, but what was most important to Chris and me was going back to HUP. It had been over a year since I had left and I was anxious to make an appearance. However, my confidence was impaired. I could not make a simple phone call to arrange a meeting with any of the people who had helped me back to life. It was too overwhelming. I had become very conscious of my delayed responses and speech problems. I was apprehensive and decided against a planned reunion with all the people who had helped me through my ordeal in 1993. I thought it would be better to simply drop-in unannounced, so we stopped by HUP one afternoon.

I was looking forward to seeing the doctors, Diane, Adam, Christine or any of the familiar faces that I had been thinking about...and dreaming about... and constantly remembering from my days as an inpatient. But, no one knew of my plan to visit.

Diane had left HUP only a week earlier and had moved to Pittsburgh, four hours away. It was Adam's day off. But, I did see Christine, my OT... and Melissa, one of the first post-coma therapists... and Dolly, one of the nurses who had been there during my illness.

My old room was vacant, so I went in. How bittersweet I felt, clearly remembering noises, and voices... and feelings It was amazing how that one room had become my world. Now, it was quiet. Unusually serene.

Chris, Elizabeth and I took the elevator down to the fifth floor hoping to see Dr. Kotapka. It was a shot in the dark. I hadn't called... he was probably in surgery. Kelly, his assistant, was most pleasant, as always. Kelly amazed me. Her responsibilities were immense, yet she made it all look like a stroll in the park. She made a few phone calls and informed us Dr. Kotapka was just out of surgery and would be there soon. I didn't want to rush him. I know that if it was me he was working on, I wouldn't want him to rush. Kelly reassured us.

After 10 minutes, Dr. Kotapka entered the room and after greeting the three of us he directed us to a vacant office. Usually, I had great difficulty speaking, always losing the thought of what I want to say the moment I open my mouth to speak. The short-term memory deficit. But, not this time. Something came over me, I couldn't stop talking. I wanted him to know all that I remembered from the awakening to the final surgery, but only my interactions with *him*. It was my responsibility to tell him for the sake of "medicine", and for all those stuck inside themselves as I had been. I thanked him for saving my life. Dr. Kotapka simply said there was *someone else* involved... that he had only done what he was trained to do in medical school. I had always been so practical, I had never been able to fully understand, or *believe* in a higher power. But, at that moment, a reevaluation began in my mind.

Dr. Kotapka let Elizabeth have free reign of the room and she quickly found interest in a slide container, removing the contents without hesitation. Chris and I apologized. Dr. Kotapka laughed and gave her the empty container as a souvenir.

After awhile, Dr. Langer came by. All of us reminisced about that day, Sunday, December 27, 1992. Dr. Kotapka had been buying tires on City Line Avenue when his beeper sounded. Dr. Lasner was in the ER. Chris was in our apartment in Maine, when he received the long-distance call. And, Elizabeth and I were at The Hospital of the University of Pennsylvania, too.

~ ~ ~ ~ ~ ~

Dr.

There was nothing.

One day in the life that was mine
          and the child within me,
It all stopped... and suddenly,

There was nothing.

There were warnings,
But the warnings remained silent...
In this busy... busy... busy world.

In what was my mind,
Stirrings began.
Initially, they were vague memories,
          ...but they clung.
Like a skier on a bottomless mountain,
Slowly... ever so slowly,
They grabbed onto the hand of my mind,
And I pulled those memories up with me

Not knowing how to tie my shoelaces,
          or write my name,
          or eat,
At least I could blink... and I could see.

And you came in one time.
I knew you were someone important in my
          new life.

But it was so utterly confusing,
          and sad...
          and sad.
The more I thought the sadder I became,
But the sadness just kept inspiring me
To remember my life.

October 1994 in therapy at Bayside, I was told to start a journal and write in it everyday. I wasn't able to do that with my responsibilities at home, coupled with the delays of my new mind. The therapists had no interest in my excuses. So, I began *taping* my daily routine with a micro-cassette recorder. As I worked on the stair-stepper, I played it back. I would hear the speech difficulties as well as attention breakdowns. It took three days to figure-out how to use the micro-cassette.

My therapist at Bayside asked me to design a playhouse for Elizabeth as a project in therapy. It was a matter of tapping into areas in my mind to retrieve information. I sat at my drafting table and began trying make sense of the tools which were once so familiar to me and the knowledge that had been my life.

The first drawing was pretty basic and I saw a problem with perspective right-off. So, I began another sketch... then another. It was happening so quickly, like a slow but steady leak in the walls of a sand castle. I felt silent rushes of knowledge, like waves in my mind. I couldn't believe it was happening so deliberately, but I was so grateful.

After two hours, I had completed the rough draft of the playhouse. The following couple weeks, were the architectural drawings. It was a major hurdle in the track back to my former self... and I didn't stumble. I glided over it.

November 27, 1994

The thing about a brain injury, are the subtleties. The subtle things that used to make up "Madeleine." There are fleeting memories of what I used to do, or be. Little things, or kind gestures... writing a note to a friend. It's not something I think about doing anymore. It's not something I do anymore because the minute I think about it, I can't remember what it was that I was just going to do. The thought of the kind gesture is gone.

(14 minutes)

The holidays were approaching once again. Another year had passed since the bleed and I needed a break from therapy. In mid-November 1994, I announced I was to end therapy until after the new year. Up to this point, I had listened to Chris's advice about everything in my life, because I felt it was necessary. I was tired of the constant race against the clock, my days were a blur for the circumstances under which I was existing. Due to the effects of the bleed, I didn't have the sense to realize that the pressure was too much. My days were not just about raising a little one, that would be normal, as all my friends and family were in the same boat. For me, it was also keeping up with therapy and dealing with the problems of post AVM bleed. It was creating tension between Chris and me. Chris was still driving me everywhere, it was time to regain my independence by learning to drive again. Chris didn't agree. Although, I relied on his insight to help me get back to who I had been, suddenly something in my soul said *time to fly on my own.* I made an appointment with the Maine Head Trauma Center in Bangor, for a driving evaluation.

December 1994 and January 1995, I learned to drive again in and around our neighborhood. I could clearly see that my Accord five-speed was not going to cut it anymore. *Shifting* was dangerous because of the delays in my reactions, so I sold my old Honda and bought a used Honda automatic. Chris, Elizabeth and I drove up to Bangor for the evaluation. We spent the night at the *Holiday Inn* and at 10:00 AM the next day I began the test. The exam consisted of a combination written/visual test, using a video-tape simulation. Afterwards, I was to drive accompanied by three instructors which is always character building. Just to get out of the parking lot was enough for me, I was ready to call-it-a-day because I was so nervous. The instructors had me drive around the city. I was vaguely familiar with some areas as I had been there once before as a representative of the architectural firm in a bidding competition in 1988. Everywhere I was told to drive, memories of my days as a representative of the firm flooded my mind. Finally, I was told to yield to enter the highway.

The primary instructor was a woman from Southeastern Pennsylvania, the very town where my late first husband lived. It seems no matter where you go in this world there are always connections.

I received the results of the evaluation the following week

with the recommendation of another month of monitored driving. At the end of January, I contacted Bayside to complete my therapy. It made such a difference being able to drive again. People in this country take so much for granted every day... I took so much for granted. But now, after two years, I regained my ability to drive a car.

~ ~ ~ ~ ~ ~

Since I had come back to Bayside, there were scheduling problems. Either the therapist or I would change the time or day of my session. One day I showed-up two hours early and I didn't know quite what to do with myself. I went to the bathroom to evaluate the situation and decided to take advantage of the free time by driving to get coffee. It seemed a good task and one that I could handle.

I drove around, but found myself getting farther and farther from any familiar place. So, I pulled off to the side of the road and told myself not to become disoriented. *Go back to where you came, and try again*, I said to myself. So I did, and it happened again. This time the roads led to *Old Port*, which is the dock area and also the boutique center of the city. Once again, I parked to gather my wits and got out of the car to walk.

After a half-hour, I had to get a handle on the situation. It wasn't a big deal as long as I didn't make it one. I finally got the coffee that I set out for to begin with. I visualized the route back to Bayside and got in the car. I got back to the building a couple of minutes late, but in one piece. My life had become a series of situations; every hour was a situation. It wasn't anything new that I would become disoriented or forgetful. So, when I made it back that day, *in one piece*, it was small victory.

By mid-May, after two years, my therapy at Bayside was completed.

~ ~ ~ ~ ~ ~

Finally, after four years, I can stir my coffee and put the lid back on the sugar at the same time. That, is what I took for granted.

10

The Last Particle

Since waking from the coma, everything in my life was void of security. Watching or listening to the news of the world left me feeling terrified. Terrorist bombings, nuclear threats, rape, murder... all of the horror that is life had become my own private nightmare. All of the personal injustices that I had encountered in my own life were always in the forefront of my mind. I knew what needed to be done. I hoped I'd be able to pull myself out of the "whirlpool" that is brain injury. I felt the improvements but it was difficult knowing exactly where I stood in my recovery.

There was a man Chris and I knew who had a stroke in 1993, he was in his fifties. When I heard of this, I wondered how he was doing as the months passed. I thought perhaps the man we knew was improving as I had. Until one day Chris received the news that the man had committed suicide. At first, I said *"Why?"*, but then I remembered those days at HUP, Magee and Bayside. I remembered waking from the coma and then I felt the tremendous "weight of the world" that had come down on me as it had everyday throughout the recovery. I thoroughly remembered those days. I never, *ever* thought I would overcome what had happened. Even the second year after the bleed, still my mind raced, and raced, and raced. I began to realize I may *never recover*.

Then, in August 1995, two years and eight months after

the bleed, I noticed something was different. *The racing had stopped.* Finally, after two years and eight months, my brain was at peace. I just sat there thinking, *This is it...*

I closed my eyes and whispered, "Thank you, God."

I hadn't framed the Interior Business Design award since I had received it in 1990, so I did. At the same time, I framed Elizabeth's first drawing and Chris's Realtor's license, as suddenly I realized the importance of recognition of our accomplishments in our lives.

I began working on a watercolor painting in August 1995, in the hope that I would be able to complete it in time for a visit with Dr. Kotapka and his wife, in October. Unfortunately, the meeting was canceled at the last minute, as he was called back to the ER. I received the message at our hotel, through voice mail. I could hear the disappointment in his tone, but I didn't mind. After all, there was a life to save that day just as he had saved mine on December 27, 1992. I dropped the painting off at his office at HUP the next day and we had a brief encounter before he was called back to his duties. I told him the painting was the least I could do for him as an indication of what *he* had given back to *me*.

~ ~ ~ ~ ~ ~

As I have done the entirety of my life, I've rarely been satisfied with the completion of a task. There is always a sense of *"I could have done better..."* Perhaps that is the soul of an artist. In the same light, I couldn't rest until my post AVM therapy was completed in May 1995. Now, it's the completion of this story, not for the story's sake, but for those who may benefit from it.

Often times, the injustice of being "brain-injured" has forced me into silence. Ironic, after the fight to communicate for so long. In the struggle to find myself again, I have been faced with ignorance and prejudice, but I have tried to rise above it. I didn't want to become obsessed by it. The difficulty has been keeping the conflict within. It wears me down and undermines my capabilities. I find myself covering my mouth in conversations, involuntarily. Of course, a lot of people do that. In my case, it's not with my hand that I cover my mouth, it's with my fist.

My life is no different than anyone's. I was born... grew-up...had difficulties... made mistakes on the way... learned... married... had a child. I'm just a person in this world. I've had tragedies too, perhaps more than most but that wasn't what I planned. It wasn't what I wanted. I didn't have the *strength* many times in my recovery. I didn't have the knowledge, but fortunately, I had someone in my life pulling me up from the hole I was in. I saw the injustices of it all and that made me fight even harder. I wanted to be on the outside looking in again. I'm on the outside now but it was a long journey.

Maybe, it's a matter of recognizing the value of a life. The importance of family and friends, and the need to rise above the imperfections of those participating in one's life. Every recollection of moments in my life... of the people who built my memories, has become so invaluable... because it is my life. It all has meaning now. The thing is, people who have had an ordeal such as mine and are lucky enough to function in life again, are few and far between. The general public is caught in the web of life and my story becomes just that... a story. But, maybe I can catch someone's interest and perhaps there will be hope in someone's life if they read this. Every single life has such significance. *Does everyone know that?*

I don't dream anymore but I have a feeling it will happen soon. In February 1995 I told myself to wake up at 4:AM, just to see if my mind had the ability to follow a command... and at 4:AM the next morning, I woke. For those who may not understand the significance, those who have had a traumatic brain injury usually sleep pretty soundly, like drinking a bottle of *Jack Daniel's* before bed. In this case, there was no alarm and no cues. It was *just me, myself and I.* As if to reconfirm that triumph, I woke at the same exact time the following morning!

I'm painting again and was invited to exhibit in a gallery in Ogunquit summer 1995 and 1996. During the summer of 1996, I tried jogging, too. After three years of fast walking, I put my *fear of falling* aside and I was able to run. It was a bit much for my system though, as the following morning I was unable to move my right side. But, shortly thereafter, I regained a substantial amount of feeling in my right leg. One step back... two steps forward.

In September 1996, I was hired to do a set of architectural plans for a builder in Kennebunk, Maine. It will be another five years before I can come close to working as I once did. I'm a Mom now, you see.

I'd like to say it was all just a terrible nightmare and finally, I've woken up... but that's not what happened. It's not enough to say that I'm just the same as before but that I've gone *beyond* who I was. Now I see the path so clearly. It seems there is absolutely no way that I'm ever going to lose sight of it again... *but you never know*. The AVM is gone, although I still have problems with short-term memory and brain fatigue, as well as mathematical problems, reading aloud, and a plethora of minor physical "leftovers" from the bleed. I may not be in the 99.95 % in mechanical reasoning as I had been, I don't know... but, cognitively I'm pretty close to home. Physically, my system has sprung back from the *twisting* it had done that was so perplexing to all of the doctors I had seen. Gradually, my mind has settled down once again. Now, it's just my psyche that is trying to come to terms with what has happened. My feeling is everything is going to be just fine... better than fine.

When I woke from the coma, in that moment there was a *presence* within me. It wasn't anything I was looking for... it was just there. *"I had been laid there and something was with me"*, I thought on January 31, 1993. I didn't even know my name at that point. Still, *something* was with me. It was the only thing *alive* in my mind and it wasn't until what could have been my final hour that this was revealed to me. But, it has taken a new level of awareness to understand what it was. As I was completing this story in the hope that it would serve as inspiration for others, suddenly I realized what that something was. I began to make connections of the moments in my life when I was left in the dark... a life without meaning. I began to see clearly, *"why things are the way they are"*, and I began to understand what the gift of life is. It was something that was given to me when I was sick, but I think it had *always* been there. All the hard times I had experienced in my own life, had lead me to this place. Just like a clearing in the forest... and I found it.

The *indescribable entity* that I had awakened to on January 31, 1993, *is God*... and it is in *me*. I didn't recognize God that day. It wasn't until one day in February 1996 that I put it all together.

In the blink of an eye, I was given knowledge that I had

never known... and it wouldn't stop. I was overwhelmed at the clarity I was given and at first, it frightened me. I had found the needle in the haystack. I opened a door and discovered a whole new universe, one that changed my way of thinking... and of being. Suddenly, I understood that which I hadn't. My mind peeled away the layers of pain and confusion and ignorance. It was constant, it calmed my fears and it was the only thing that mattered. It was the rope that pulled me up. I felt sad for who I had been but I realized this was the beginning of my new life.

In the days and weeks that followed this revelation, I had multitudes of awakenings. The encountering has given me insight that I never had and also a fear that I never had. I have been humbled. In my life, I have been waiting for a sign of what God is. It was the last particle of my being and it *shimmered*... like a light. It was a strong beacon that never wavered. I didn't know what it was, only that it was in me... and it was the only thing left. Within me, and with everything that has happened in my life, I found something *extraordinary*. I can only say, something was given to me and I knew what it was.

It went on for a few weeks and gradually I was no longer afraid but rather, accepting. My life has been a search for God, as is true of many people... but to actually see the light... *experience the light*, was my gift of recovery and of **life**.

~ ~ ~ ~ ~ ~

I thought that was it. I thought I had figured it out: *God is in me*. But, something else was knocking at the door, something other than the gift of my life.

Suddenly, I realized... it was not just *me*. My recovery had to do with a soul, but not *my* soul. It was the smallest soul. The selfless, unaffected, innocent happy soul of the child within my body. It was so clear. *Carved in stone* in my mind, and in that moment I understood. It was Elizabeth who pulled all of us through. I will forever be so grateful to Chris for his decisions concerning the little soul within my body while I was comatose and incapacitated. It was the smallest soul.

Everyday of my recovery I tended to Elizabeth, I wouldn't have it any other way. People thought I was incapable of taking care of my child, but they were wrong. I changed her diapers... I bathed her... I sung to her... I laughed with her... I held her and I'm still doing it. My bond...*our* bond with our child, is what life *is*. It put everything in perspective, again.

That day, December 27, 1992, everything changed in my life, for a long time. *Forever.* I lost myself but slowly found a different version of me. It seems more than anyone could have hoped for... but, isn't that life? Now, it all comes down to being happy again. It's pretty basic. Happiness is being with Chris and Elizabeth, my family. Family is life. Change is life. It's always been that way, too.

~ ~ ~ ~ ~ ~

What is true is that we ourselves are more than however much we strive to achieve. What is false is that losing anything will be the end of us. What is true is that losing something can, in fact, be the beginning of an exciting new world, a totally new life, a completely different and even more satisfying way of being. What is real is that the water at the source and the water downstream are not two different natures. Whatever we are when our great life changes come is what we shall take into the next phase of life."

Joan Chittister

In our backyard in Maine stands a forest of trees; peaceful, untainted and void of the disturbances of city dwelling. When the sun is up and if it's not cloudy I can see the back of the woods extending another thousand feet. The significance of this scene is an analogy not unlike my own saga... knowing something was wrong but unable to find the answer. Each time I see the sun breaking through the branches I try to see how far my eyes will take me. It's as if it's not enough... I always want to see the forest through the trees. In my mind, the forest never ends because I reached the back of the forest one day... but it wasn't my time. It wasn't in the plan.

All the moments in my life, I've searched for the right path. I guess, that is what life is all about. You never know the impact you may have on someone. You may think you will just bumble through life doing whatever it is that you do until, one day something changes. If you're lucky, you get a second chance at *doing life*. You may see things differently as if through a new pair of eyes. If that happens, you may say to yourself... *"I'm going to it right this time."*

Becoming

You are left with nothing.

The awareness of your nothingness
Has not yet been revealed.

When you begin to comprehend,
You embark on the pilgrimage
That will lead to your destiny.

If your will is strong enough,
or if you have someone
to cause your will to be strong,
Suddenly you can see
So clearly.

Much more clearly than
You've ever seen before.

Your priorities change,
Your views change,
Your beliefs reach up into a higher place...
and you realize.

GLOSSARY

GLOSSARY

---

antibiotic : any of certain substances, as penecillin or streptomycin, produced by some microorganisms and capable of destroying or weakening bacteria.

arterio : a learned borrowing from the greek meaning artery used in the formation of compound words.

arteriovenous : of or pertaining to an artery and vein.

aphasia : loss of power to use or understand words.

bronchitis : inflammation of the membrane lining of the bronchial tubes.

craniotomy : the operation of opening the skull, usually for operations on the brain.

diuretic : increasing the volume of urine as by a medical substance

embolism : the obstruction of a blood vessel as by blood clot or air bubble.

hemorrage : to bleed profusely; a discharge of blood, as from a ruptured blood vessel.

harbinger : a forerunner; herald.

hydrocephalus : an accumulation of serous fluid within the cranium, often causing great enlargement of the head.

insulin : a hormone produced by the islets of Langerhans of the pancreas that regulates the metabolism of glucose and other carbohydrates.

ICH : intracranial hemorrage.

intracranial : being within the cranium or skull.

I.V. : intravenous: directly into a vein.

malformation : faulty or anomalous formation or structure, especially in a living body.

morphine : A white, bitter, crystalline alkaloid, the most important narcotic principle of opium, obtained by extraction and crystallization: used chiefly in medicine in the form of its sulfate, hydrochloride, or in other salt to dull pain, as a sedative and to induce sleep.

neurology : the science of the nerves and the nervous system, especially of the diseases affecting them.

O.T. (occupational therapy) : therapy consisting of light work, such as basketry, carpentry, etc. that provides mental diversion and frequently serves to exercise an affected part of the body or give vocational training.

overtone : an additional usually, subsidiary and implicit, meaning or quality.

otorhinolaryngology : scientific study of ear/nose/throat.

P.T. (physical therapy) : physiotherapy

phenobarbital : used as a sedative, a hypnotic, and as an antispasmodic in epilepsy.

pulmonary : of or pertaining to the lungs.

shunt : to divert blood by means of a shunt by moving it or turning it to one side.

speech pathology (speech therapy) : the scientific study and treatment of deficits, disorders, and malfunctions of speech and voice and of language disturbances, as aphasia, delayed language acquisition, etc.

supine : lying on the back, or with the face or front upward.

transfusion : the direct transferring of blood from one person or animal to another.

tracheostomy : the formation of an artificial opening, either permanent or semi-permanent, into the trachea.

ventricle : one of a series of connecting cavities of the brain.

ventricular : of, pertaining to, of the nature of a ventricle of or pertaining to a belly or something resembling one.

ventriquolostomy : the formation of a drain for cerebrospinal fluid from the ventricle of the brain.

ventilate (ventilator) : to expose blood to air in the lungs in respiration: oxygenate.

zygoma : *(anatomy)* a bone on each side of the face below the eye, forming the pronouncement of the cheek and part of the orbit. Also called *malar, malar bone, cheekbone.*